The Heart
of Chinese
Poetry

Also by Greg Whincup

REDISCOVERING THE I CHING

The Heart of Chinese Poetry

Greg Whincup

ANCHOR PRESS
Doubleday
NEW YORK
1987

Library of Congress Cataloging-in-Publication Data

The Heart of Chinese poetry.

Bibliography: p. 175
1. Chinese poetry—Translations into English.
2. English poetry—Translations from Chinese.   I. Whincup,
Gregory.
PL2658.E3H35   1987   895.1'1'008   86-29143

ISBN 0-385-23966-1 (hardcover)
      0-385-23967-x (paper)
Calligraphy by South China Arts, Victoria, B.C.

To the memory of R. H. Blyth,
whose books on Japanese haiku
first showed me the heart of poetry

Preface

Poetry was queen of the arts in traditional China. Every educated person wrote verses, and the best poets of any age were great celebrities.

Why was poetry such a passion? The only way I can really answer that question is by trying to kindle the same passion in you.

The aim of this book is to make fifty-seven of the greatest Chinese poems come alive for Western readers. It presents the poems in a new way that brings the reader face to face with their original Chinese texts, and with the worlds of the poets who wrote them.

This is a book to be read for enjoyment. As you dip into it, however, you will find yourself picking up quite a bit of information about Chinese poetry, Chinese culture, and even about the Chinese language.

I hope that you will come to feel that none of these are alien. Inasmuch as we are all members of one human race, Chinese culture is our culture. Poetry is the heart of Chinese culture. The heart of Chinese poetry beats in us, too.

For their comments on various parts of the manuscript, I would like to thank Jean Rockwell, Greg Hollingshead, Charles Douglas, Ruth Wilson, Paul Wilson, Ben Stewart, Elling O. Eide, and Sheila Whincup. I apologize for not adopting more of their suggestions.

I would also like to thank my editor Susan Schwartz and my agent Deborah Schneider for all they have done.

GREG WHINCUP
Sooke, Vancouver Island
October 1986

A Note about Pronunciation

Chinese pronunciations are given in the Yale system of romanization. This system was developed specifically for teaching Chinese to Americans. Though not widely used, it is the only system that allows untrained readers to come reasonably close to proper Chinese pronunciation.

The most important thing to remember is that each Chinese word is pronounced as one syllable: *mau* is not like "may you" but like the "mou" in "mouse."

Further details are given on page 173.

Proper names are written in the Chinese way, surname first and given name second—for example, Li Bai, Li Ching-jau.

Poems

流水窅然去別有天地非人間

問余何意棲碧山笑而不答心自閑桃花

山中問答　李白

The Heart of Chinese Poetry

1. Question and Answer in the Mountains

Ask me
Why I stay
On Green Mountain?
I smile
And do not answer,
My heart is at ease.

Peach blossoms
On flowing water
Slip away
Into the distance—
This is another world
Which is not of men.

LI BAI 李白
Tang Dynasty
About 730 A.D.

1 wèn　問 ASK
yú　余 ME
hé　何 WHAT
yì　意 IDEA
chī　棲 ROOST
Bì　碧 GREEN
Shān　山 MOUNTAIN?

2 syàu　笑 SMILE
ér　而 AND
bù　不 NOT
dá　答 REPLY,
syīn　心 HEART
dż　自 OF ITSELF
syén　閑 AT EASE

3 táu　桃 PEACH
hwā　花 BLOSSOM
lyóu　流 FLOWING
shwěi　水 WATER,
yǎu　宵 DISTANT-
rán　然 -LY
chyù　去 GOES

4 byé　別 ANOTHER
yǒu　有 THERE IS
tyēn　天 HEAVEN
dì　地 EARTH,
fēi　非 NOT

Chinese poems are like strings of jewels.

The jewels are Chinese characters, each of which represents a one-syllable word.

These little word-jewels are hard and unchanging, but when they are translated into English, each one seems to have several different meanings.

The word 山 *shan*, for example, can mean "mountain" or "mountains."

The word 笑 *syau* can mean "a smile," "smiling" or "to smile."

In fact, 山 and 笑 do not really have more than one meaning. It is just that their meaning is broader than any one English word.

The heart of the jewel never changes, but its surface reflects the light in many different ways.

LI BAI (701–762 A.D.) was the most sublimely talented of all Chinese poets. He was like

rén	人	PEOPLE
jyēn	間	AMONG

a god, or a force of nature.

He accepted no restrictions in his life, but floated through China making poetry and spending time with nature and his friends.

When he wrote this poem he was living in the hills of central China, in a place he compares to the mythical earthly paradise, PEACH BLOSSOM SPRING 桃花源 .

Words which rhyme are *italicized* in the pronunciation column at the left-hand side of the page.

2. *Traveling at Night*

Slender grasses,
A breeze on the riverbank,
The tall mast
Of my boat alone in the night.

Stars hang
All across a vast plain.
The moon leaps
In the Great River's flow.

My writing
Has not made a name for me,
And now, due to age and illness,
I must quit my official post.

Floating on the wind,
What do I resemble?
A solitary gull
Between the heavens and the earth.

DU FU 杜甫
Tang Dynasty
765 A.D.

1	syì	細	FINE
	tsău	草	GRASS,
	wēi	微	TINY
	fēng	風	WIND
	àn	岸	SHORE
2	wēi	危	TOWERING
	chyáng	檣	MAST,
	dú	獨	SOLITARY
	yè	夜	NIGHT
	jōu	舟	BOAT
3	syīng	星	STARS
	chwéi	垂	HANG DOWN,
	píng	平	LEVEL
	yĕ	野	WILDS
	kwò	闊	BROAD
4	ywè	月	MOON
	yŭng	湧	LEAPS,
	dà	大	GREAT
	jyāng	江	RIVER
	lyóu	流	FLOWS
5	míng	名	NAME,
	chĭ	豈	HOW
	wén	文	LITERARY
	jāng	章	PIECES
	jù	著	ESTABLISH?
6	gwān	官	OFFICE,
	yīng	應	MUST

The essence of Chinese poetry is emotion linked to landscape. Chinese poets make the natural world an expression of human emotion.

This is more than just a literary convention. The unity of man and nature is part of the traditional Chinese perception of the world.

In the West, we think of the Chinese as an unemotional people. This is far from true. Within the family or among friends, they express emotions of great depth and intensity. Such emotions are expressed publicly in poetry.

When he wrote this poem, DU FU (712–770 A.D.) was a middle-aged man of fifty-three. His poetry was not much appreciated and his patron had just died, forcing Du to pack up his family and move on.

He felt very insecure—like a blade of grass bending in the breeze, a solitary boat in the night, the moon's reflection tossed about in the water, a single gull lost in the sky.

If only he had known. He

	lǎu	老	OLD
	bìng	病	ILL
	syōu	休	QUIT
7	pyāu	飄	FLOATING
	pyāu	飄	FLOATING,
	hé	何	WHAT
	swǒ	所	THAT WHICH
	sż	似	RESEMBLE?
8	tyēn	天	HEAVEN
	dì	地	EARTH,
	yī	一	ONE
	shā	沙	SAND
	ōu	鷗	GULL

and his friend Li Bai have been revered for a thousand years as China's greatest poets.

Li's easy brilliance is contrasted with Du's craftsmanship, Li's mysticism with Du's deep moral passion for events in the world. In a way, Du is the Beethoven to Li's playful Mozart.

HEAVEN AND EARTH 天地 means "the world."

The SAND GULL 沙鷗 is a species of gull.

Du Fu's name is usually written in English as "Tu Fu," Li Bai's as "Li Po."

3. *Thinking of Past Wanderings*

Li Bai wrote a poem
About West of the Waters
Temple.
Ancient trees,
Encircling peaks,
The wind through high rooms.

Half-sober,
Half-drunk,
I wandered there three days.
Red, white,
Flowers opened
In the mountain rain.

> Du Mu 杜牧
> Tang Dynasty
> About 830 A.D.

1	Lǐ	李	LI
	Bái	白	BAI
	tí	題	WROTE
	shř	詩	POEM
	Shwěi	水	WATER
	Syī	西	WEST
	Sż	寺	TEMPLE
2	gǔ	古	ANCIENT
	mù	木	TREES,
	hwéi	回	ENCIRCLING
	yén	巖	PEAKS,
	lóu	樓	HIGH BUILD-INGS
	gé	閣	COVERED GAL-LERIES
	fēng	風	WIND
3	bàn	半	HALF
	syǐng	醒	SOBER,
	bàn	半	HALF
	dzwèi	醉	DRUNK,
	yóu	游	WANDERED
	sān	三	THREE
	ř	日	DAYS
4	húng	紅	RED
	bái	白	WHITE
	hwā	花	FLOWERS
	kāi	開	OPENED,

Classical Chinese poetry was basically a means of expressing emotion. But it became as well a means of liberation from emotion.

In imposing their emotions on the natural world, Chinese poets became more and more integrated with it. This in turn gave nature the opportunity to impose itself on them.

It showed them the reality that their emotions obscured: things just are as they are—the flowers just open, the rain just falls. Emotions are beside the point.

West of the Waters Temple was famous for its covered galleries, perched high above a mountain stream. Du Mu (803–852 A.D.) visited the temple about a century after the great Li Bai had been there.

In his poem, Li Bai had written:

Clear and quick
Sings the twisting stream.
Among green bamboos
Wind flying galleries.

shān	山	MOUNTAIN
yǔ	雨	RAIN
jūng	中	AMID

Do not confuse Du Mu with Li Bai's contemporary Du Fu, who also had the surname Du:

Dù Fù 杜甫 c. 730 A.D.
Dù Mù 杜牧 c. 830 A.D.

江南春　　杜牧

千里鶯啼綠映紅水村山郭酒旗風南朝
四百八十寺多少樓臺煙雨中

The History of Chinese Poetry

4. *In the Wilds There Are Creepers*

In the wilds
There are creepers,
The dewfall
Lies in droplets, oh!

A beautiful person,
Her clear brow
So lovely, oh!

We happen to meet.
She is just what
I desire, oh!

In the wilds
There are creepers,
The dewfall lies thick.

A beautiful person,
Lovely her clear brow.

We happen to meet:
"To be with you
Is good."

> Book of Songs 詩經
> Jou Dynasty
> Before 500 B.C.

野 *Outlying Land*　蔓 *Creeper*
有 *There Are*　草 *Plants*

1	yĕ	野	OUTLYING LAND
	yŏu	有	THERE ARE
	màn	蔓	CREEPER
	tsău	草	PLANTS
2	líng	零	FALLEN
	lù	露	DEW
	twán	溥	IN DROPLETS
	syī	兮	OH!
3	yŏu	有	THERE IS
	mĕi	美	BEAUTIFUL
	yī	一	ONE
	rén	人	PERSON
4	chīng	清	CLEAR
	yáng	揚	BROW
	wăn	婉	IS LOVELY
	syī	兮	OH!
5	syè	邂	BY HAPPY CHANCE
	hòu	逅	
	syāng	相	EACH OTHER
	yù	遇	MEET
6	shĭ	適	SUITS
	wŏ	我	MY
	ywàn	願	DESIRE
	syī	兮	OH!

The next nine poems trace the history of Chinese poetry, from ancient times down to around 1200 A.D.

Chinese poetry begins with the Book of Songs, a collection of hymns and folk songs composed between about 1000 and 600 B.C.

These songs have a strangeness and simplicity that make them seem the voices of another world. And that in fact is just what they are—the voices of the Chinese Bronze Age.

ONE 一 is the simplest of all Chinese characters. "Two" is written 二 and "three" 三 .

PERSON 人 is the simplest possible stick figure of a human being.

Few characters are so simple, however. Most are combinations of two or more separate elements:

EACH OTHER	相 = 木 + 目	
MEET	遇 = 辶 + 禺	
DESIRE	願 = 原 + 頁	
DEW	露 = 雨 + 足 + 各	
PLANTS	草 = 艹 + 早	

7 yĕ	野	OUTLYING LAND
yŏu	有	THERE ARE
màn	蔓	CREEPER
tsău	草	PLANTS
8 líng	零	FALLEN
lù	露	DEW
ráng	瀼	THICK
ráng	瀼	THICK
9 yŏu	有	THERE IS
mĕi	美	BEAUTIFUL
yī	一	ONE
rén	人	PERSON
10 wăn	婉	LOVELY
rú	如	-LIKE
chīng	清	CLEAR
yáng	揚	BROW
11 syè	邂	BY HAPPY
hòu	逅	CHANCE
syāng	相	EACH OTHER
yù	遇	MEET
12 yŭ	與	"WITH
dž	子	YOU
jye	偕	TO BE TO-GETHER
dzāng	臧	IS GOOD"

Each of these elements has a sound and a meaning of its own, and could be written as a separate character.

Most characters are made up of two elements, basing their meaning on one and taking their sound from the other.

For instance, the word 清 *ching* CLEAR is made up of 氵 "water" and 青, the sound *ching*.

So 清 is a word pronounced *ching* (青) that has something to do with water (氵). It originally described clear water, but came to be used for anything clear.

Several related words often have the same pronunciation, and are written using the same sound-element with a different meaning-element:

清 *ching* "clear" =
氵 "water" + 青 *ching*
情 *ching* "feelings" =
忄 "heart" + 青 *ching*
晴 *ching* "clear sky" =
日 "sun" + 青 *ching*

The element 青 *ching* itself means "green," but Chinese readers do not think of this when they see 清 or 情 or 晴

5. The Autumn Wind

The autumn wind rises,
White clouds fly.
Plants brown and withered,
Geese return south.

Orchids in bloom,
Chrysanthemums fragrant.
I cherish a fair one
I cannot forget.

We sail a high boat
To cross the Fen River.
Crossing in mid current
We rise on the white waves.

Pipes and drums sound,
An oar song is sung,
Though pleasure's at its peak
Sad feelings arise:

Hale youth cannot last,
There's no stop for old age.

Emperor Wu　漢武帝
Han Dynasty
About 100 B.C.

秋 *Autumn*
風 *Wind*
辭 *Composition*

1 chyōu	秋	AUTUMN
fēng	風	WIND
chǐ	起	RISES
syī	兮	OH!
bái	白	WHITE
yún	雲	CLOUDS
fēi	飛	FLY
2 tsǎu	草	PLANTS
mù	木	TREES
hwáng	黃	BROWN
lwò	落	FALLING
syī	兮	OH!
yèn	雁	WILD GEESE
nán	南	SOUTH
gwēi	歸	RETURN
3 lán	蘭	ORCHIDS
yǒu	有	HAVE
syòu	秀	BLOSSOMS
syī	兮	OH!
jyú	菊	CHRYSANTHE-MUMS
yǒu	有	HAVE
fāng	芳	FRAGRANCE
4 hwái	懷	CHERISH
jyā	佳	FAIR
rén	人	PERSON
syī	兮	OH!
bù	不	NOT

The Han Dynasty (about 200 B.C.–200 A.D.) was the end of ancient China and the beginning of the imperial age.

This song retains some of the freshness of the Book of Songs, but is richer and more complex.

Between 500 and 200 B.C., China passed through a crucible of chaos and war. The old feudal order boiled away. Philosophers like Confucius and Lao-tzu tried to reconstruct a moral and intellectual order for the new world that was emerging. In the process, they raised Chinese thought to a new level of sophistication.

By the time this poem was written, around 100 B.C., China had enjoyed unity and peace for about a century. The Han Dynasty was at the peak of its power.

Like its near contemporary the Roman Empire, the Han Dynasty wove the cultural patterns of the ancient world into a new fabric that would endure for two thousand years.

néng	能	CAN
wáng	忘	FORGET
5 fàn	汎	FLOAT
lóu	樓	STORIED
chwán	船	BOAT
syī	兮	OH!
jì	濟	CROSS
Fén	汾	FEN
Hé	河	RIVER
6 héng	橫	CUT ACROSS
jūng	中	MID
lyóu	流	FLOW
syī	兮	OH!
yáng	揚	LIFT
sù	素	WHITE
bwō	波	WAVES
7 syāu	蕭	PIPES
gǔ	鼓	DRUMS
míng	鳴	SING
syī	兮	OH!
fā	發	PUT FORTH
jàu	櫂	OAR
gē	歌	SONG
8 hwān	歡	DELIGHT
lè	樂	PLEASURE
jí	極	EXTREME
syī	兮	OH!
āi	哀	GRIEF
chíng	情	FEELINGS
dwō	多	MANY
9 shàu	少	YOUTH
jwàng	壯	VIGOR
jǐ	幾	HOW MUCH
shŕ	時	TIME

The Chinese still call themselves "People of Han."

Lines 5 and 6 describe boating on the river. Many of the words in them include the element 氵 "water":

汎	FLOAT	濟	CROSS
汾	FEN	河	RIVER
流	FLOW	波	WAVES

But looking at a Chinese character is like looking at a face. You do not notice the individual features, you get an overall impression of who the person is and what he's like.

When you look at the character 汎 you get an impression of floating, and of the sound *fan*, you do not notice 氵 "water" and 凡 *fan*.

Emperor WU (reigned 140–86 B.C.) was one of the greatest of all Chinese emperors. He expanded the empire into Korea, Central Asia, and Vietnam. He was a patron of the arts. And it was he who first established the Confucian classics as the basis of Chinese education.

Unfortunately, his grandiose palaces and great military expeditions left the government bankrupt, and sent the dynasty into decline.

The poem ends on a note of hopeless foreboding that is common in Han poetry. No

syī	兮 OH!	Han philosophy had a satisfy-
nài	奈 PREVENT	ing answer to the problem of
lău	老 OLD AGE	death, and life after death.
hé	何 HOW?	This began to change only cen-

Han philosophy had a satisfying answer to the problem of death, and life after death. This began to change only centuries later, when Indian Buddhism became naturalized in China.

6. *Expressing My Feelings*

In the night
I cannot sleep.
I rise and sit
To play the singing lute.

Through light curtains
I watch the bright moon.
A fresh breeze
Blows at my clothes.

A solitary wild goose
Calls in the wilderness.
Circling birds
Cry in the northern woods.

Fretting and pacing,
What is it I expect to see?
With sadness and grief
I am alone.

RWAN JI 阮籍
Wei Dynasty
About 250 A.D.

1 yè	夜	NIGHT
jūng	中	-WITHIN,
bù	不	NOT
néng	能	ABLE TO
mèi	寐	SLEEP
2 chǐ	起	ARISE
dzwò	座	SIT DOWN,
tán	彈	PLAY
míng	鳴	SINGING
chín	琴	LUTE
3 báu	薄	THIN
wéi	惟	CURTAINS,
jyèn	鑒	SEE IMAGE OF
míng	明	BRIGHT
ywè	月	MOON
4 chīng	輕	LIGHT
fēng	風	WIND
chwēi	吹	BLOWS
wǒ	我	MY
jīn	襟	LAPEL
5 gū	孤	SOLITARY
húng	鴻	WILD GOOSE
hàu	號	CALLS
wài	外	OUTER
yě	野	WILDS
6 syáng	翔	CIRCLING
nyǎu	鳥	BIRDS
míng	鳴	CRY

After ruling China for four centuries, the Han Dynasty finally fell around 200 A.D. China sank once again into disunity and war.

RWAN JI (210–263 A.D.) was one of the "Seven Sages of the Bamboo Grove," a group of prominent intellectuals who had given up on the disheartening and dangerous politics of the day.

The Seven Sages and their followers met in a bamboo grove outside the capital for philosophical discussions enlivened by music and wine.

MOON 月 . Every Chinese character has a history. Before 1000 B.C., the word MOON was written ☽ . This evolved into ☽ and then, around 200 B.C., into the modern form, 月 .

Rwan Ji had apparently abandoned politics, but he still had political opinions, and expressed them covertly in his poems. The WILD GOOSE alone in the wilderness may be Rwan himself. The BIRDS in the northern woods may be the clique in power in the capital.

23

	běi	北	NORTHERN
	lín	林	WOODS
7	pái	徘	PACING BACK
	hwái	徊	AND FORTH,
	jyāng	將	ABOUT TO
	hé	何	WHAT
	jyèn	見	SEE?
8	yōu	憂	SORROWFUL
	sz̄	思	LONGING,
	dú	獨	ALONE
	shāng	傷	WOUNDED
	syīn	心	HEART

BIRDS 鳥 is a simplified drawing of a bird. Its ancient form was 帚

CRY 鳴 is a mouth 口 beside a bird 鳥.

WOODS 林 is two trees standing side by side.

Some Chinese words have more than one syllable. Because *pai-hwai* PACING BACK AND FORTH has two syllables, it is written with two characters, 徘徊.

7. "Lady Night" Song of Spring

The spring woods
Hold flowers of much loveliness.
Spring birds
Cause thoughts of much woe.

The spring breeze
Has much amorous feeling.
It blows open
My light silken skirt.

Anonymous
Six Dynasties Period
300–600 A.D.

子 *Lady*   時 *Seasons*
夜 *Night*   歌 *Song*
四 *Four*   春 *of Spring*

1 chwūn   春 SPRING
   lín   林 WOODS,
   hwā   花 FLOWERS
   dwō   多 MUCH
   méi   媚 LOVELINESS

2 chwūn   春 SPRING
   nyǎu   鳥 BIRDS,
   yì   意 THOUGHTS
   dwō   多 MUCH
   āi   哀 GRIEF

3 chwūn   春 SPRING
   fēng   風 WIND
   fù   復 ALSO
   dwō   多 MUCH
   chíng   情 FEELING

4 chwēi   吹 BLOWS
   wǒ   我 MY
   lwó   羅 GAUZE SILK
   cháng   裳 SKIRT
   kāi   開 OPEN

The "Lady Night" songs were popular songs of the Six Dynasties period, about 300–600 A.D.

A mysterious woman known as *Dž-yè* 子夜 "Lady Night" or "Midnight" is said to have composed and sung the first of them, but many more were written over the years.

Their playful eroticism reflects the life of the leisured classes in southern China at the time.

Politically, the country had fallen apart. Northern China was divided among a number of rulers. Dynasties came and went quickly in the south.

Despite the political chaos, the southern gentry still managed to lead a life of ease and pleasure.

In this poem, nature is so infused with human feeling that it becomes personified, in the amorous breeze.

8. On a Tour of the Fields, I Climb the Mountain on Serpentine Island, at the Mouth of the Sea

The traveler's sorrow
What can console?
To gaze upon the sea
And rest on the winds of dawn.

None can distinguish
The limit of the broad waves.
Who knows what lies
To the east of the ocean?

I seem to hear a song
Of the pleasures of boating.
A smile starts to wreathe
My sorrowful face.

I will wander the jasper-green sands
Of the islands,
And roam
The cinnabar-red peaks.

SYE LING-YUN 謝靈運
Six Dynasties Period
Probably 423 A.D.

行	*Travel*	口	*-Mouth*
田	*Fields*	盤	*Serpentine*
登	*Climb*	嶼	*Islet*
海	*Sea-*	山	*Mountain*

1	jī	羈	SOJOURNER'S
	kŭ	苦	BITTER SOR-ROWS,
	shú	孰	WHAT
	yún	云	SAY
	wèi	慰	CONSOLE?
2	gwān	觀	GAZE AT
	hăi	海	SEA,
	jyè	藉	TAKE COM-FORT FROM
	jāu	朝	DAWN
	fēng	風	WIND
3	mwò	莫	NO ONE
	byèn	辨	DISTIN-GUISHES
	húng	洪	VAST
	bwō	波	WAVES'
	jí	極	LIMIT
4	shwéi	誰	WHO
	jř	知	KNOWS
	dà	大	GREAT
	hwò	壑	DEEPS
	dūng	東	EAST?
5	yī	依	AS IF
	syī	稀	

SYE LING-YUN (385–433 A.D.) was China's first great landscape poet.

He came from one of southern China's most powerful families. In his youth, he was a well-known dandy and a celebrity in fashionable literary circles.

But he joined the wrong political faction and, at the age of thirty-three, was exiled to a remote region of the southeastern coast. It was there he began writing the poems of "mountain and water" that have made him famous.

Sye had already studied both native Chinese mystical Taoism and the Indian Buddhism that was then becoming naturalized in China.

His exile deepened his interest in religion. He became a believer in the "sudden enlightenment" school of Buddhism, a forerunner of Zen.

The Six Dynasties period was an era of political despair.

Tsăi	採	"PICKING
Líng	菱	WATER
		CHESTNUTS
Gē	歌	SONG"
6 făng	彷	SEEMS TO
fú	佛	
hán	含	HOLD CON-
		TAINED
pín	頻	KNITTED
		BROW
rúng	容	FACIAL
		EXPRESSION
7 áu	遨	RAMBLE
yóu	遊	WANDER
bì	碧	JASPER-GREEN
shā	沙	SAND
jŭ	諸	ISLANDS
8 yóu	遊	WANDER
yĕn	衍	ON AND ON
dān	丹	CINNABAR-
		RED
shān	山	MOUNTAIN
fēng	峯	PEAKS

Many of those with the means to do so retreated into either pleasure or religion.

Both Taoists and Buddhists sought freedom in the natural world. Taoists became solitary recluses, Buddhists built monasteries in the mountains. There they gained intuitions of nature that Sye and others made into the basis of China's great tradition of nature poetry.

The PICKING WATER CHEST-NUTS SONG 採菱歌 (translated "a song of the pleasures of boating" in the verse translation of the poem) was a popular ballad about boating and love. Versions of it were sung on aristocratic pleasure-boating expeditions around the capital, from which Sye had been exiled.

9. Seeing Off a Friend

Green mountains
Lie across the northern outskirts
Of the city.
White water
Winds around the eastern
City wall.

Once we make our parting
Here in this place,
Like a solitary tumbleweed
You will go
Ten thousand miles.

Floating clouds
Are the thoughts of the wanderer.
Setting sun
Is the mood of his old friend.

With a wave of the hand
Now you go from here.
Your horse gives a whinny
As it departs.

> LI BAI 李白
> Tang Dynasty
> About 750 A.D.

送
友
人

*Seeing Off
Friend-
-Person*

1	chīng	青	GREEN
	shān	山	MOUNTAINS
	héng	横	LIE ACROSS
	běi	北	NORTHERN
	gwō	郭	OUTSKIRTS
2	bái	白	WHITE
	shwěi	水	WATER
	rǎu	繞	WINDS AROUND
	dūng	東	EASTERN
	chéng	城	CITY WALL
3	tsž	此	THIS
	dì	地	GROUND,
	yī	一	ONCE
	wéi	爲	MAKE
	byé	別	PARTING
4	gū	孤	SOLITARY
	péng	蓬	TUMBLEWEED
	wàn	萬	TEN THOUSAND
	lǐ	里	MILES
	jēng	征	MARCH
5	fú	浮	FLOATING
	yún	雲	CLOUDS,
	yóu	游	WANDER-
	dž	子	-ER'S
	yì	意	THOUGHTS

The years from about 700 to 750 A.D. were the golden age of Chinese poetry. China's two greatest poets—Li Bai and Du Fu—shone brightest in a constellation of poetic stars.

By 700 A.D., northern and southern China had been reunited under the Tang Dynasty for about a century. Their union now gave birth to a culture with the martial strength of the north and the elegance of the south.

Some of the robust clarity of the verse of this "High Tang" period comes from its use of parallelism. Notice how each word in line 1 has an exact parallel in line 2:

GREEN // WHITE
MOUNTAINS // WATER
LIE ACROSS // WINDS AROUND
NORTHERN // EASTERN
OUTSKIRTS // CITY WALL

In almost all Chinese poetry, each pair of lines is a separate unit, almost like a stanza. Pairs that are parallel gain an emphasis that makes them the

6	lwò	落	FALLING
	r̀	日	SUN,
	gù	故	OLD
	rén	人	FRIEND'S
	chíng	情	FEELINGS
7	hwēi	揮	WAVE
	shǒu	手	HAND,
	dż	自	FROM
	dž	茲	THIS
	chyù	去	GO
8	syāu	蕭	SYAU
	syāu	蕭	SYAU,
	bān	班	SEPARATED
	mǎ	馬	HORSE
	míng	鳴	CRIES

solid pegs on which the rest of the poem hangs.

Here, lines 1–2 are parallel, lines 3–4 are not. Lines 5–6 again are parallel, lines 7–8 are not.

The strong, emotion-laden images of the parallel lines 5–6 (FLOATING CLOUDS, FALLING SUN) are the heart of the poem. Lines 7–8 trail away to the final parting.

TEN THOUSAND MILES 萬里 (line 4) is poetic overstatement. In any case, the old Chinese "mile" or *li* 里 was equal to only one-third of a standard mile, or half a kilometer.

OLD FRIEND (line 6) is literally "old person" 故人 .This is "old" in the sense not of "aged," but rather "of long standing."

10. *Southern Spring*

A thousand miles
Of caroling warblers,
Flowers that flash red
Against the green.
Villages by the water
And walled mountain-towns,
Wine-shop banners in the breeze.

Four hundred eighty
Temples of the Southern Dynasties:
How many high buildings
In the mist and rain?

Du Mu 杜牧
Tang Dynasty
About 830 A.D.

江 *River-*
南 *-South*
春 *Spring*

1	chyēn	千 THOUSAND
	lǐ	里 MILES
	yīng	鶯 WARBLERS
	tí	啼 SING,
	lyù	綠 GREEN
	yìng	映 FLASHES
	húng	紅 RED
2	shwěi	水 WATER
	tswēn	村 VILLAGE
	shān	山 MOUNTAIN
	gwō	郭 WALLED TOWN,
	jyǒu	酒 WINE
	chí	旗 BANNERS
	fēng	風 WIND
3	Nán	南 SOUTHERN
	Cháu	朝 DYNASTIES
	sż	四 FOUR
	bǎi	百 HUNDRED
	bā	八 EIGHTY
	shŕ	十
	sż	寺 TEMPLES
4	dwō	多 HOW MANY
	shǎu	少
	lóu	樓 HIGH
	tái	臺 BUILDINGS
	yēn	煙 MIST

Du Mu (803–852 A.D.) lived almost a century after the golden age of Tang poetry. His poems are incomparably rich and vivid, but the strength of a hundred years before is gone.

RIVER-SOUTH 江南 is the region south of the lower reaches of the Yangtze River in southeastern China. Its climate and its culture are still the most luxurious in China.

FLASHES 映 is made up of 日 "sun" plus a sound-element 央 .

WINE BANNERS 酒旗 were flags hung on tall poles as the sign of a wine-shop.

The SOUTHERN DYNASTIES 南朝 were the short-lived last four of the Six Dynasties, covering the period from about 400–600 A.D. Their capitals were all at what is now Nanking, in the heart of the "South of the River" region. temples were built at that time, during the first flowering of Buddhism in China.

yŭ　　雨 RAIN
jŭng　　中 AMID?

EIGHTY is literally "eight tens" 八十 .

HOW MANY is literally "many-few" 多少 .

HIGH BUILDINGS is "storied buildings" 樓 and "towers" 臺 .

11. Written on the Wall
of North Tower after Snow

In the evening,
It was still raining fine threads.
But the night
Was calm and windless,
And things turned more severe.

I felt only
That the bedclothes
Had been spattered with moisture.
I did not know
The courtyard
Was heaped up with salt.

In the hour before dawn
The look of morning came
Through the curtains of my study.
The half-moon
With a cold sound
Dropped from painted eaves.

As I tried to sweep
North Tower, I looked up
At Horse-Ears Peak:
All that was not buried
Were two tips.

Su Shr 蘇軾
Northern Sung Dynasty
1074 A.D.

雪 *Snow*　　臺 *Tower*
後 *after*　　書 *Write on*
北 *North*　　壁 *Wall*

1	hwáng	黃	YELLOW
	hwūn	昏	DUSK
	yóu	猶	STILL
	dzwò	作	MAKING
	yǔ	雨	RAIN
	syēn	纖	FINE
	syēn	纖	FINE
2	yè	夜	NIGHT
	jìng	靜	CALM
	wú	無	WITHOUT
	fēng	風	WIND,
	shr̀	勢	SITUATION
	jwǎn	轉	TURNED
	yén	嚴	SEVERE
3	dàn	但	ONLY
	jywé	覺	FELT
	chīn	衾	BED-
	chóu	裯	-CLOTHES
	rú	如	AS IF
	pwō	潑	SPATTERED
	shwěi	水	WATER
4	bù	不	NOT
	jr̄	知	KNOW
	tíng	庭	COURTYARD
	ywàn	院	
	yǐ	已	ALREADY
	dwēi	堆	HEAPED
	yén	鹽	SALT

The Tang Dynasty finally fell about 900 A.D. Fifty years later, the Sung Dynasty rose in its place.

Sung was a less passionate, more philosophical era than Tang. The favorite drink of Tang China was wine. It was during the Sung Dynasty that tea first became popular. Many Sung poems have the pale astringence of Chinese tea.

To WRITE ON THE WALL 書壁 may seem strange, but it was perfectly normal for a well-known poet to take up the brush and write a poem on the whitewashed wall of an inn or a temple or his own house.

TURNED 轉 is made up of 車 "carriage" and 專 *jwan*. The archetype of turning is a carriage wheel.

SU SHR (1036–1101 A.D.) was the greatest of Sung poets. And he was not only a great poet, but a great essayist, a great calligrapher, a well-known painter, a kindly and effective local administrator, a forthright critic of government

5	wǔ	五	FIFTH
	gēng	更	WATCH
	syǎu	曉	DAWN
	sè	色	COLOR
	lái	來	CAME TO
	shū	書	STUDY
	hwǎng	恍	CURTAINS

6	bàn	半	HALF
	ywè	月	MOON
	hán	寒	COLD
	shēng	聲	SOUND
	lwò	落	FELL FROM
	hwà	畫	PAINTED
	yén	簷	EAVES

7	shř	試	TRIED
	sǎu	掃	SWEEP
	Běi	北	NORTH
	Tái	臺	TOWER,
	kàn	看	SAW
	Mǎ	馬	HORSE
	Ěr	耳	EARS

8	wèi	未	HAD NOT
	swéi	隨	FOLLOWED
	mái	埋	BURIED
	mwò	沒	SUNK,
	yǒu	有	THERE WERE
	shwāng	雙	PAIR OF
	jyēn	尖	TIPS

policy, and a Zen Buddhist who attained some degree of enlightenment.

Because of its swift, easy pace, Su's poetry has been compared to "a fine horse speeding through the air."

In old China, the night was divided into five two-hour "watches." The FIFTH WATCH 五更 came just before dawn.

STUDY is literally "book" 書 .

The COLD SOUND 寒聲 Su refers to is probably the cold hush caused by a heavy snowfall. Some commentators think it is the crack of a frozen rooftile.

The EAVES 簷 of the grand building he was staying in were PAINTED 畫 with bright designs.

When he wrote this poem, Su had just taken up residence as governor of Mi-jou in Shantung province, northeastern China. NORTH TOWER 北臺 was in the government compound there, against the north wall of the town.

HORSE EARS 馬耳 is a peak south of the town of Mi-jou.

The matter-of-fact, almost pedestrian tone of the poem is common in Sung poetry. It may be a result of the Sung revival of humanist Confucianism, or of the Buddhist realization that there is enlightenment in everyday life.

12. *I Want to Go Out,*
but It's Raining

The east wind blows rain,
Vexing the rambler.
The road turns to mud
From fine dust.

Flowers sleep, willows drowse,
Spring itself is lazy.
And it turns out that I
Am even lazier than spring.

Lu You 陸游
Southern Sung Dynasty
About 1200 A.D.

1	dūng	東 EAST
	fēng	風 WIND
	chwēi	吹 BLOWS
	yŭ	雨 RAIN,
	nău	惱 VEXES
	yóu	游 WANDERING
	rén	人 PERSON
2	măn	滿 ENTIRE
	lù	路 ROAD
	syīn	新 NEW
	ní	泥 MUD
	hwàn	換 REPLACES
	syì	細 FINE
	chén	塵 DUST
3	hwā	花 FLOWERS
	shwèi	睡 SLEEP
	lyŏu	柳 WILLOWS
	myén	眠 DROWSE,
	chwūn	春 SPRING
	dż	自 ITSELF
	lăn	懶 IS LAZY
4	shwéi	誰 WHO
	jř	知 KNEW
	wŏ	我 I
	gèng	更 EVEN MORE
	lăn	懶 LAZY
	rú	如 THAN
	chwūn	春 SPRING?

Until the Sung Dynasty, most Chinese poetry is sad. With Sung, however, comes a mood of acceptance and of quirky humor.

LU YOU (1125–1210 A.D.) was the most prolific of all Chinese poets. When his long, peaceful life ended, he left behind him over ten thousand poems.

Lu lived during the Southern Sung Period (about 1100–1300 A.D.). The Golden Tartars had seized control of northern China, but the Sung Dynasty retained power in the south, which enjoyed two centuries of peace and plenty.

Both 睡 SLEEP and 眠 DROWSE contain the element 目 "eye."

SELF 自 looks a lot like 目 "eye." In fact, however, the ancient form of 自 "self" was a picture of a nose 𦣻.

Even today, when Chinese people point to themselves, they point to the nose, not to the chest, as English-speaking people do.

Notice that the character 春 SPRING contains the element 日 "sun."

Three Poets of the Golden Age

春望　　杜甫

國破山河在城春草木深感時花濺淚

恨別鳥驚心烽火連三月家書抵萬金

白頭搔更短渾欲不勝簪

13. *Spring Sunrise*

Slumbering in spring,
Unaware of sunrise,
Everywhere around me
I hear the twittering of birds.

In the night
Came sounds of wind and rain.
Flowers fell—
I wonder how many?

MENG HAU-RAN 孟浩然
Tang Dynasty
About 725 A.D.

1	chwūn	春	SPRING
	myén	眠	SLEEPING,
	bù	不	NOT
	jywé	覺	AWARE OF
	syău	曉	SUNRISE
3	chù	處	EVERY-
	chù	處	-WHERE
	wén	聞	HEAR
	tí	啼	TWITTERING
	nyău	鳥	BIRDS
4	yè	夜	NIGHT
	lái	來	CAME
	fēng	風	WIND
	yŭ	雨	RAIN
	shēng	聲	SOUND
5	hwā	花	FLOWERS
	lwò	落	FELL,
	jŕ	知	KNOW
	dwō	多	HOW MANY?
	shău	少	

We now turn back from the late 1100s A.D. to the early 700s, to take a closer look at three poets of the golden age of Tang—Meng Hau-ran, Li Bai, and Du Fu.

MENG HAU-RAN (689–740 A.D.) helped create the role of the irresponsible Tang counter-culture poet. He spent much of his life in retirement on his small estate in the hills, yet still managed to become friendly with the greatest poets of his time, including LI BAI.

EVERYWHERE is literally "place-place 處處 ."

Each line of a Chinese poem falls naturally into two or more separate phrases. In five-word lines like these, the division is normally after the second word—for example:

Line 1 SPRING SLEEPING
       NOT AWARE SUNRISE
Line 2 PLACE PLACE
       HEAR TWITTERING BIRDS

14. *In the Evening of the Year,*
I Return to the Southern Mountains

I abandon
My supplications
To the northern palace towers,
And return
To my humble cottage
In the southern mountains.

Because I have no talent,
The Glorious Ruler has dropped me
My illnesses are many
And my friends are few.

White hair
Urges on old age.
The sunny green of spring
Hurries these last days of the year.

Always brooding
On my sorrows, I cannot sleep.
Moon in the pines
Through my window empty in the night.

MENG HAU-RAN 孟浩然
Tang Dynasty
729 A.D.

歲 *Year's*　　南 *Southern*
暮 *Evening*　　山 *Mountains*
歸 *Return to*

1	běi	北 NORTHERN
	chywè	闕 PALACE
		TOWERS,
	syōu	休 CEASE
	shàng	上 SENDING UP
	shū	書 LETTERS
2	nán	南 SOUTHERN
	shān	山 MOUNTAINS,
	gwēi	歸 RETURN TO
	bì	敝 HUMBLE
	lú	廬 COTTAGE
3	bù	不 NOT
	tsái	才 TALENTED,
	míng	明 SHINING
	jǔ	主 RULER
	chì	棄 ABANDONED
4	dwō	多 MANY
	bìng	病 ILLNESSES,
	gù	故 FRIENDS
	rén	人
	shū	疏 SPARSE
5	bái	白 WHITE
	fǎ	髮 HAIR
	tswēi	催 URGES ON
	nyén	年 YEARS
	lǎu	老 OLD

In late 727 A.D., at the age of thirty-eight, MENG HAU-RAN left his home in the southern mountains and traveled north to the capital to try the civil service examination. He failed.

This was a hard blow. An older man competing against boys fifteen or twenty years younger and losing—losing a chance to gain the public respect that only government service could bring.

There is a famous anecdote about MENG's stay in the capital. It is almost certainly untrue, but I am going to tell it anyway:

The younger poet Wang Wei held a post in the palace and Meng was visiting him one day when the emperor arrived unexpectedly. In panic, Meng scrambled under a bed to hide, but Wang was unwilling to conceal him from the emperor, and forced him to come out.

The emperor was delighted to meet such a well-known poet, and commanded him to

6 chīng	青	GREEN
yáng	陽	SUNNINESS
bī	逼	PRESSES
swèi	歲	YEAR'S
yú	餘	REMAINDER
7 yǔng	永	ALWAYS
hwái	懷	BROODING,
chóu	愁	SORROWFUL
bù	不	NOT
mèi	寐	SLEEP
8 sūng	松	PINES
ywè	月	MOON,
yè	夜	NIGHT
chwāng	窗	WINDOW
syū	虛	EMPTY

recite a poem. In his confusion, he recited this one.

At the line, "The Glorious Ruler has dropped me," the emperor was not amused. "I have never dropped you," he said angrily. "How could I, since you have never applied to me for a position?" And he ordered him to leave the capital and go home.

Almost all Chinese words dealing with the emotions contain the element 心 "heart." In 愁 SORROWFUL, the heart is obvious. However, in 懷 BROODING the alternative form 忄, the "standing heart," is used. Both 心 and 忄 are descended from the ancient form 心, which looks somewhat more like a heart.

15. Written for Old Friends in Yang-jou City While Spending the Night on the Tung-lu River

I hear the apes howl sadly
In dark mountains.
The blue river
Flows swiftly through the night.

The wind cries
In the leaves on either bank.
The moon shines
On a solitary boat.

These wild hills
Are not my country.
I think of past ramblings
In the city with you.

I will take
These two lines of tears,
And send them to you
Far away
At the western reach of the sea.

MENG HAU-RAN 孟浩然
Tang Dynasty
Early 730s A.D.

宿 *Staying Overnight*
桐 *Tung-*　　　　　廣 *Gwang-*
廬 *-lu*　　　　　　陵 *-ling*
江 *River,*　　　　舊 *Old*
寄 *Sent to*　　　　遊 *Ramblers*

1	shān	山	MOUNTAINS
	mìng	暝	NIGHT,
	tìng	聽	HEAR
	ywán	猿	APES
	chóu	愁	SAD

2	tsāng	蒼	BLUE
	jyāng	江	RIVER
	jí	急	QUICKLY
	yè	夜	NIGHT
	lyóu	流	FLOWS

3	fēng	風	WIND
	míng	鳴	CRIES
	lyǎng	兩	TWO
	àn	岸	RIVERBANKS'
	yè	葉	LEAVES

4	ywè	月	MOON
	jàu	照	SHINES ON
	yī	一	ONE
	gū	孤	SOLITARY
	jōu	舟	BOAT

5	Jyèn	建	JYEN
	Dé	德	DE
	fēi	非	IS NOT

Perhaps because he lived alone, MENG HAU-RAN particularly cherished his friends.

In the early 730s, after failing the government examination, he traveled extensively in southeastern China, visiting his friends there and viewing all the scenic places.

The TUNG-LU RIVER 桐廬江 flows through the wooded hills of JYEN-DE 建德 county in the interior of Chekiang province.

GWANG-LING 廣陵 is an old name for the city of Yang-jou. Yang-jou was the Paris of Tang China: the great city of both culture and pleasure.

Notice how this poem is constructed:

Lines 1–2 set the scene—night on the river among the hills.
Lines 3–4 continue with more detail—wind, leaves, moon, boat.
Lines 5–6 specifically introduce

wú	吾	MY
tŭ	土	LAND
6 Wéi	維	WEI
Yáng	揚	YANG
yì	憶	REMEMBER
jyòu	舊	OLD
yóu	遊	RAMBLERS
7 hwán	還	AGAIN
jyāng	將	TAKE
lyăng	兩	TWO
háng	行	LINES
lèi	淚	TEARS
8 yáu	遙	DISTANT
jì	寄	SEND TO
hăi	海	SEA'S
syī	西	WESTERN
tóu	頭	HEAD

the poet's feelings—he feels lonely and alien.

Finally, lines 7–8 tie the poem together—the poet declares his love for his friends.

You can find this same general pattern in many poems:

1: Introduction
2: Continuing detail
3: Some special twist of thought or feeling
4: Conclusion.

Looking for this pattern will often make the shape of a poem come clear.

WEI-YANG 維揚 ("the city" in the verse translation) is another old name for Yang-jou.

WESTERN HEAD 西頭 ("western reach") alludes to the fact that Yang-jou lies up the Yangtze River westward from the sea.

16. For Meng Hau-ran

I love Master Meng.
Free as the flowing breeze,
He is famous
Throughout the world.

In rosy youth, he cast away
Official cap and carriage.
Now, a white-haired elder, he reclines
Amid pines and cloud.

Drunk beneath the moon,
He often attains sagehood.
Lost among the flowers,
He serves no lord.

How can I aspire
To such a high mountain?
Here below, to his clear fragrance
I bow.

Li Bai 李白
Tang Dynasty
About 730 A.D.

1 wú　　吾　I
　ài　　愛　LOVE
　Mèng　孟　MENG
　Fū　　夫　MASTER
　Dž　　子

2 fēng　　風　WIND-
　lyóu　　流　-FLOW,
　tyēn　　天　HEAVEN-
　syà　　下　-BENEATH
　wén　　聞　FAMOUS

3 húng　　紅　RED
　yén　　顏　COMPLEXION,
　chì　　棄　ABANDONED
　sywān　軒　CARRIAGE
　myěn　　冕　CAP

4 bái　　白　WHITE
　shǒu　　首　HEAD,
　wò　　臥　LIES
　sūng　　松　PINES
　yún　　雲　CLOUDS

5 dzwèi　醉　DRUNK
　ywè　　月　MOON,
　pín　　頻　OFTEN
　jūng　　中　ATTAINS
　shèng　聖　SAGEHOOD

6 mí　　迷　BEDAZZLED
　hwā　　花　FLOWERS,

The unconventional Li Bai loved Meng Hau-ran for his unconventionality. Meng was fourteen years older. To Li, his life was a model one, based entirely on poetry, friendship, and drink.

WIND-FLOW 風流 ("free as the flowing breeze") is a beautiful but elusive expression that has variously been translated "elegant and free," "talented and unconventional," "distinguished," "stylish," "attractive," "dissipated," and "gay." Today, it is sometimes applied to film stars.

HEAVEN-BENEATH 天下 means "everywhere under Heaven," which is to say "throughout China," or "throughout the world."

RED COMPLEXION 紅顏 means "rosy youth."

CARRIAGE and CAP 軒冕 were signs of official rank: a chauffeured carriage and a cap of office.

The word 中 ATTAIN means to hit a target. The phrase 中聖 "hit sagehood" can also mean "be hit by the sage."

bù	不	NOT	
shỉ	事	SERVE	
jyūn	君	LORD	
7 gāu	高	HIGH	
shān	山	MOUNTAIN,	
ān	安	HOW	
kě	可	CAN	
yǎng	仰	ASPIRE TO?	
8 tú	徒	IN VAIN	
tsž	此	HERE	
yī	揖	BOW TO	
chīng	清	CLEAR	
fēn	芬	FRAGRANCE	

"The sage" was drinkers' slang for fine wine.

BEDAZZLED 迷 literally means "lost" or "confused."

Meng Hau-ran was a famous drinker. A government official once offered to introduce him at court, where he might get a position as a court poet.

But when the time came for him to go, a friend happened by, and they fell to drinking and talking. "Hadn't you better be on your way?" asked the friend after a while.

"Oh, why bother," replied Meng, "My job is to drink and enjoy myself."

17. At Yellow Crane Tower, Seeing Off Meng Hau-ran on His Way to Yang-jou

My old friend
Bids farewell to me
In the west at Yellow Crane Tower.
Amid April's mist and flowers
He goes down to Yang-jou.

The distant image
Of his lonely sail
Disappears in blue emptiness,
And all I see
Is the Long River
Flowing to the edge of sky.

LI BAI 李白
Tang Dynasty
About 730 A.D.

黄 *Yellow* 浩 *Hau-*
鶴 *Crane* 然 *-ran*
樓 *Tower* 之 *Going to*
送 *Send Off* 廣 *Gwang-*
孟 *Meng* 陵 *-ling*

1	gù	故	OLD
	rén	人	FRIEND
	syī	西	WEST
	tśz	辭	LEAVES
	Hwáng	黄	YELLOW
	Hè	鶴	CRANE
	Lóu	樓	TOWER
2	yēn	煙	MIST
	hwā	花	FLOWERS
	sān	三	THIRD
	ywè	月	MONTH
	syà	下	GOES DOWN
	Yáng	揚	YANG
	Jōu	州	JOU
3	gū	孤	LONELY
	fān	帆	SAIL
	ywǎn	遠	DISTANT
	yǐng	影	SHADOW,
	bì	碧	BLUE
	kūng	空	EMPTINESS
	jìn	盡	DISAPPEARS
4	wéi	惟	ONLY
	jyèn	見	SEE
	Cháng	長	LONG
	Jyāng	江	RIVER,

For many reasons, this is one of LI BAI's most famous poems: its flowing sound and structure; its beautiful imagery and grand scale; its association with famous people and places; and its poignant but indirect expression of love for a friend.

A reconstruction of the YELLOW CRANE TOWER 黄鶴樓 still affords a panoramic view of the junction of the Yangtze and Han rivers in central China.

Meng had sailed south down the Han from his retreat in the hills. He was about to continue eastward down the Yangtze to the city of YANG-JOU (also called GWANG-LING) four hundred miles away. Li had probably come a hundred miles from his own retreat to meet his friend and send him on his way.

The traditional Chinese year, which is based on phases of the moon, usually begins in

tyēn	天 HEAVEN'S
jì	際 EDGE
lyóu	流 FLOWING

our February. The THIRD MONTH 三月 , therefore, begins in April and continues into May.

This poem flows with the waters of the Yangtze, from Yellow Crane Tower (line 1), to the departure of Meng's boat (line 2), to the boat's disappearance against the sky (line 3), to the river flowing on alone (line 4).

LONG RIVER 長江 is the Chinese name for the Yangtze. "Yangtze" is the name of a small section of the river near Yang-jou.

18. A Song of Heng-jyang

After the sea-spirit passes,
An evil wind swirls.
Waves batter Heaven's Gate,
The cliff cracks open.

How could the tide
On the River Je
In September equal this?
Waves like a range of mountains come,
Spitting snow.

LI BAI 李白
Tang Dynasty
About 750 A.D.

1 hǎi   海 SEA
  (húy)

shén 神 SPIRIT
  (jīn)

lái   來 COME
  (lūy)

gwò 過 PASSED,
  (gwàh)

è   惡 EVIL
  (ahk)

fēng 風 WIND
  (byūhng)

hwéi 回 SWIRLS
  (*hwūy*)

2 làng 浪 ROUGH
  (làhng)   WAVES

dǎ   打 HIT
  (dá)

tyēn 天 HEAVEN'S
  (tāyn)

mén 門 GATE,
  (mūn)

shŕ   石 STONE
  (zhyak)

bì   壁 WALL
  (bayk)

kāi 開 OPENS
  (*kūy*)

The supernatural was a natural part of Li Bai's world.

HENG-JYANG 橫江 was a ferry-crossing on the Yangtze, about thirty miles upstream from Nanking.

You may have noticed that in some poems, the italicized words, which are supposed to rhyme, do not. Although Chinese characters have remained the same in the thousand years since most of these poems were written, the way they are pronounced has changed.

Modern linguists have reconstructed what they think is a good approximation of Tang pronunciation. This is represented by the spellings in parentheses. See also poem 25 (page 77).

HEAVEN'S GATE 天門 is a mountain on the Yangtze River at Heng-jyang.

There is a powerful tidal bore on the JE RIVER 浙江 at

3 Jè 浙 JE
  (Jyèt)
  Jyāng 江 RIVER
  (Gāng)
  bā 八 EIGHTH
  (bāt)
  ywè 月 MONTH
  (ngywat)
  hé 何 HOW
  (hāh)
  rú 如 RESEMBLE
  (nyū)
  tsž 此 THIS?
  (tsí)

4 tāu 濤 BIG WAVES
  (dāu)
  sż 似 LIKE
  (zì)
  lyén 連 CONNECTED
  (lyēn)
  shān 山 MOUNTAINS,
  (shān)
  pēn 噴 SPITTING
  (pwūn)
  sywĕ 雪 SNOW
  (sywet)
  lái 來 COME
  (*lūy*)

the great southern city of Hangchow. It runs highest in the eighth month of the traditional lunar year. In 1974 there was a tide almost thirty feet high.

SPITTING 噴 does not mean to expectorate, but to spit water from your mouth in a spray.

SNOW 雪 here refers to flying spray, not to actual snow.

The violence of the Yangtze at Heng-jyang captured Li Bai's imagination. He wrote a set of six "Songs of Heng-jyang," of which this is one. And he also wrote an "Inscription on Heaven's Gate Mountain."

The inscription includes the lines: "Churning sand and flying waves, drowning horses and killing men."

19. *Amusing Myself*

Drinking,
I was unaware of nightfall.
Fallen flowers
Filled my robe.

Drunk, I arose
And walked by the stream
In the moonlight.
The birds had all gone,
Men also were few.

LI BAI 李白
Tang Dynasty
About 750 A.D.

自 *Myself*
遣 *Whiling Away Time*

1 dwèi	對	FACING
jyŏu	酒	WINE,
bù	不	NOT
jywé	覺	AWARE OF
mìng	暝	NIGHT
2 lwò	落	FALLEN
hwā	花	FLOWERS
yíng	盈	FILLED TO OVERFLOW- ING
wŏ	我	MY
yī	衣	CLOTHES
3 dzwèi	醉	DRUNK
chĭ	起	AROSE,
bù	步	WALKED
syī	溪	STREAM
ywè	月	MOON
4 nyău	鳥	BIRDS
hwán	還	RETURNED,
rén	人	PEOPLE
yì	亦	ALSO
syī	稀	FEW

LI BAI did what he liked. Fortunately, because of his vast talent and enormous capacity for joy, friends and relatives were willing to support him throughout his life.

He grew up in the western Chinese province of Szechwan, but his ancestors were probably only partly Chinese. As a youth, he wandered off into the mountains to study the magic arts with Taoist masters.

He was a big man, reflecting the non-Chinese side of his ancestry, and was a capable swordsman in his younger days. He had a great capacity for drink, and used alcohol to gain visions of the magical world he always knew was there.

It is said that he died by falling from a boat into the water, trying to embrace the reflection of the moon.

20. Setting Out Early from White Emperor City

At dawn
We leave White Emperor,
High among colored clouds,
Returning to the lowlands,
A thousand miles in a day.

From both banks
Of the river,
The gibbons' howling never stops.
But the light boat
Has already passed ten thousand
Layered peaks.

> Li Bai 李白
> Tang Dynasty
> 759 A.D.

1	jāu	朝	DAWN
	tsź	辭	LEAVE
	Bái	白	WHITE
	Dì	帝	EMPEROR,
	tsǎi	彩	COLORED
	yún	雲	CLOUDS
	jyēn	間	AMONG
2	chyēn	千	THOUSAND
	lǐ	里	MILES
	Jyāng	江	JYANG
	Líng	陵	LING,
	yī	一	ONE
	r̀	日	DAY
	hwán	還	RETURN
3	lyǎng	兩	TWO
	àn	岸	RIVERBANKS
	ywán	猿	GIBBONS'
	shēng	聲	VOICES
	lí	啼	CRY
	bu	不	NOT
	jìn	盡	END
4	chīng	輕	LIGHT
	jōu	舟	BOAT
	yǐ	已	ALREADY
	gwò	過	PASSED
	wàn	萬	TEN THOUSAND

There is good reason for the joyful feeling of this poem: it is the song of LI BAI's return from exile.

Because of his association with a rebellious prince, he had been banished to the far southwest. He was sailing westward up the Yangtze River into exile when word reached him at White Emperor City that he had been pardoned.

WHITE EMPEROR CITY 白帝城 was a walled town on White Emperor Mountain, high above the gorges of the Yangtze in west-central China. The mountain and the city were said to have been named for a white dragon that emerged from a well there centuries before, a sign of the White Emperor, celestial ruler of the west.

JYANG-LING 江陵 ("the lowlands") is a city in the lowlands of central China, over a thousand Chinese miles east of White Emperor City down the

chúng 重 DOUBLED
shān 山 MOUNTAINS

Yangtze. The current through the gorges is so strong that a fast boat can make the trip in a day.

GIBBONS 猿 are small tree-dwelling apes that were found throughout southern China during the Tang Dynasty, but now live only in southeast Asia.

21. *Spring Prospect*

The nation
Has been destroyed,
Mountains and rivers remain.
In the city
It is spring,
Grass and trees grow deep.

Moved by the time,
Flowers blooming
Make me weep.
Resentful of separation,
Singing birds
Shock my heart.

The beacon-fires of war
Have been lit for three months now.
Ten thousand gold-pieces
I would give
For a letter from home.

My white head
I have scratched
Till it is so sparse
That soon
The hatpin
Will not hold.

Du Fu 杜甫
Tang Dynasty
757 A.D.

春 *Spring*
望 *Prospect*

1 gwó	國	NATION
pwò	破	BROKEN,
shān	山	MOUNTAINS
hé	河	RIVERS
dzài	在	REMAIN
2 chéng	城	CITY
chwūn	春	SPRING,
tsău	草	GRASS
mù	木	TREES
shēn	深	DEEP
3 gǎn	感	FEEL
shŕ	時	TIME,
hwā	花	FLOWERS
jyèn	濺	SPRINKLE
lèi	淚	TEARS
4 hèn	恨	RESENT
byé	別	SEPARATION,
nyău	鳥	BIRDS
jīng	驚	SHOCK
syīn	心	HEART
5 fēng	烽	BEACON
hwŏ	火	FIRES
lyén	連	CONTINUE
sān	三	THREE
ywè	月	MONTHS
6 jyā	家	FAMILY
shū	書	LETTER

Du Fu is ranked with Li Bai as one of China's two greatest poets. Li Bai's lightheartedness and easy flow are very different, however, from the dense craftsmanship and deep seriousness of Du Fu's verse.

Du wrote this poem in the midst of the disastrous rebellion that started the Tang Dynasty on its decline. It is his most famous poem, and lines 3–4 are two of his most famous lines:

Is it the poet who feels the time and sprinkles tears on the flowers, or do the flowers feel the time and weep drops of dew? Does "the time" refer to spring or to the rebellion? Is it the poet who is shocked or the birds?

Du ties all this up in a pair of complex, convoluted, and perfectly parallel lines. They are like a pair of matched diamonds, flashing rays of light in all directions.

Rebels took the capital, Chang-an ("Eternal Peace"), in the summer of 756 A.D., forcing the emperor to flee. That

dǐ	抵	EXCHANGE
wàn	萬	TEN THOUSAND
jīn	金	GOLD
7 bái	白	WHITE
shǒu	首	HEAD,
sāu	搔	SCRATCH
gèng	更	EVEN MORE
dwǎn	短	SHORT
8 hwún	渾	JUST ABOUT
yù	欲	WILL
bù	不	NOT
shēng	勝	ABLE TO TAKE
dzān	簪	HATPIN

fall, he abdicated in favor of his son.

Du and his wife and children fled to safety, but when he heard that the new emperor was calling for loyalists to go and join him, Du went.

On the way, he was captured by a party of rebels and taken to occupied Chang-an. He spent the winter there, among its ruined streets and untended walls, and wrote this poem as spring broke in 757.

Tang Dynasty men wore their hair bound up on top of their heads, and secured their hats to it with a long HATPIN 簪.

22. Spending the Night at the Palace Chancellery in Spring

Flowers lie hidden in the evening
By a low palace wall.
Twittering, birds
Pass over on their way to roost.

The stars
Above ten thousand doorways
Shift.
The moon's light
In the highest heaven
Is abundant.

Sitting up unsleeping
I listen for the golden lock.
On the wind
I think I hear
Bridle pendants of jade.

At dawn I will
Present a document to the emperor.
I ask several times
How far the night is spent.

DU FU 杜甫
Tang Dynasty
758 A.D.

1 hwā   花 FLOWERS
   yǐn   隱 HIDE
   yè   掖 SIDE
   ywán   坦 LOW WALL
   mù   暮 EVENING

2 jyōu   啾 JYOU
   jyōu   啾 JYOU,
   chī   棲 ROOSTING
   nyǎu   鳥 BIRDS
   gwō   過 PASS

3 syǐng   星 STARS,
   lín   臨 LOOKING
               DOWN OVER
   wàn   萬 TEN THOU-
               SAND
   hù   户 DOORWAYS
   dùng   動 MOVE

4 ywè   月 MOON,
   pàng   傍 BESIDE
   jyōu   九 NINTH
   syāu   霄 HEAVEN
   dwō   多 IS MUCH

5 bù   不 NOT
   chǐn   寢 LIE DOWN TO
               SLEEP,
   tīng   聽 LISTEN FOR
   jīn   金 GOLDEN
   yàu   鑰 LOCK

After the rebels were driven from the capital, there was a short interlude of peace and order in Du Fu's life. He was reunited with his family and for his loyalty he was rewarded with a post at court.

The LEFT DEPARTMENT 左府 ("Palace Chancellery") was the department concerned with personnel matters. Its offices were on the left-hand (east) side of the palace, which faced south.

Du's job was to make certain that no deserving official went unnoticed by the court.

The TEN THOUSAND DOOR-WAYS 萬户 are those within the vast palace.

NINTH HEAVEN 九霄 ("highest heaven") is the highest layer of the heavens. Here, however, Du is thinking of the imperial palace as the "highest heaven."

The emperor held court at dawn. Officials with presentations to make waited up all night at the palace.

The sounds of GOLDEN LOCK 金鑰 and JADE BRIDLE PEN-DANTS 玉珂 would signal the

6	yīn	因	FROM
	fēng	風	WIND,
	syǎng	想	THINK OF
	yù	玉	JADE
	kē	珂	BRIDLE PEN-
			DANTS

7	míng	明	TOMORROW
	jāu	朝	DAWN
	yǒu	有	HAVE
	fēng	封	DOCUMENT
	shř	事	TO PRESENT

8	shwò	數	SEVERAL
			TIMES
	wèn	問	ASK
	yè	夜	NIGHT
	rú	如	HOW FAR
	hé	何	ADVANCED?

emperor's arrival. Notice that the element 金 "metal," "gold," is part of 鑰 LOCK, and that 玉 "jade" is part of 珂 BRIDLE PENDANT.

DOCUMENT TO PRESENT 封事 is literally "sealed business." Documents for presentation to the emperor were sealed in black bags to prevent disclosure.

HOW FAR ADVANCED? 如何 is literally "like what?"

Du's good fortune did not last. He spoke up too strenuously for a demoted official, and was himself demoted to a post outside the capital.

23. Thinking of My Younger Brothers
on a Moonlit Night

Drums on the watchtower
Cut off men's travels.
Autumn in the borderlands—
A wild goose's cry.

The dew
Starting from tonight
Is white.
The moon
Over my old home
Is bright.

I have brothers,
But they are scattered.
There is no one to tell me
If they live or die.

The letters that I send
Never reach them.
And still,
The fighting goes on.

DU FU 杜甫
Tang Dynasty
759 A.D.

71

月 *Moon*　憶 *Remember*
夜 *Night*　舍 *Humble House*
　　　　弟 *Younger Brothers*

1	shù	戍	GUARD
	gǔ	鼓	DRUMS (*a)
	dwàn	斷	CUT OFF
	rén	人	PEOPLE'S
	syíng	行	TRAVEL
2	byēn	邊	BORDERLANDS (*a)
	chyōu	秋	AUTUMN, (*b)
	yī	一	ONE
	yèn	雁	WILD GOOSE'S
	shēng	聲	VOICE
3	lù	露	DEW, (*b)
	tsúng	從	FROM
	jīn	今	THIS
	yè	夜	NIGHT
	bái	白	WHITE (*b)
4	ywè	月	MOON, (*b)
	shř	是	IS
	gù	故	OLD
	syāng	鄉	HOMETOWN (*c)
	míng	明	BRIGHT
5	yǒu	有	HAVE
	dì	弟	YOUNGER BROTHERS, (*c)
	jyē	皆	ALL

Fighting soon broke out again. There was famine. Du quit his new post and took his wife and children west into the borderlands.

In old China, the bright autumn MOON 月 reminded people of absent friends and relatives who, wherever they were, saw the same full moon.

On cold autumn nights DEW 露 seems WHITE 白 rather than transparent.

Normally, five-word lines fall into two phrases, with the division coming after the second word—for example:

Line 1　GUARD DRUMS
　　　　CUT PEOPLE'S TRAVEL

But Du divides lines 3–4 immediately after the first word:

3　DEW
　　FROM THIS NIGHT WHITE,
4　MOON
　　IS OLD HOMETOWN BRIGHT.

Rhythmically, this gives lines 3–4 the tension of a coiled spring. The tension is released in the normal lines 5–6.

fēn	分	SEPARATED
sàn	散	SCATTERED
6 wú	無	HAVE NOT
jyā	家	FAMILY, (*c)
wèn	問	TO ASK (*d)
sž	死	DIE
shēng	生	LIVE
7 jì	寄	SEND
shū	書	LETTERS, (*d)
cháng	長	ALWAYS
bù	不	NOT
dá	達	REACH
8 kwàng	況	HOW MUCH MORE SO
nǎi	乃	THEN,
wèi	未	NOT YET
syōu	休	CEASE
bīng	兵	FIGHTING (*a)

Because Chinese is a mono-syllabic language, and because it leaves out most conjunctions, poems have a tendency to fall apart into separate phrases, lines, or couplets.

What holds them together is primarily their strictly regular rhythm and rhyme. The great craftsman Du Fu, however, also links succeeding lines by a chain of associated words and ideas (marked with asterisks *).

For example, GUARD DRUMS, BORDERLANDS, and FIGHTING (*a) would be associated in the Tang mind, as would AUTUMN, DEW, WHITE, and the full MOON (*b).

24. *Delighting in the Rain on a Spring Night*

The good rain
Knows the seasons.
It comes in the spring.

On the wind,
It infiltrates the night,
Moistening everything,
Soundless and fine.

Paths in the fields—
Dark with cloud.
Boats on the river—
Their lamps the only light.

In the morning,
There will be spots
Of wet red:
Flowers will be heavy
In the City of Brocade.

Du Fu 杜甫
Tang Dynasty
761 A.D.

1 hǎu	好	GOOD
yǔ	雨	RAIN
jř	知	KNOWS
shŕ	時	SEASONS
jyé	節	
2 dāng	當	AT
chwūn	春	SPRING,
nǎi	乃	THEN
fā	發	FORTH
shēng	生	IS BORN
3 swéi	隨	FOLLOWS
fēng	風	WIND,
chyén	潛	HIDDEN
rù	入	ENTERS
yè	夜	NIGHT
4 rwùn	潤	MOISTENS
wù	物	THINGS,
syì	細	FINE
wú	無	WITHOUT
shēng	聲	SOUND
5 yě	野	COUNTRYSIDE
jìng	徑	PATHS,
yún	雲	CLOUDS
jyū	俱	ALL
hēi	黑	BLACK
6 jyāng	江	RIVER
chwán	船	BOATS,

After only a few months in the northwestern borderlands, Du Fu and his family headed south, over the mountains, into the fertile bowl of Szechwan province. There, in the city of Chengdu, Du enjoyed the most peaceful and productive years of his life.

SEASON 時節 is literally "time-section."

Like little human figures, Chinese characters have to stand on their own feet. They must be balanced and upright and stable: not 知 but 知. All their parts must be in proportion: not 時 but 時.

HIDDEN 潛 also means "submerged." Notice the element 氵 "water."

MOISTENS 潤 is used of rain watering farmland and of a ruler showering benefits on his people.

In order to stand firmly, characters tend to have two or more legs on which to balance, and tend to open out at the bottom and close in at the top—for example:

hwǒ	火	FIRES		
dú	獨	ALONE		
míng	明	BRIGHT		
7 syǎu	曉	MORNING LIGHT		
kàn	看	SEE		
húng	紅	RED		
shř	濕	WET		
chù	處	PLACES		
8 hwā	花	FLOWERS		
jùng	重	HEAVY,		
Jīn	錦	BROCADE-		
Gwān	官	-OFFICIAL		
Chéng	城	CITY		

入 ENTER　夜 NIGHT
雨 RAIN　春 SPRING
江 RIVER　火 FIRES

If you turn these characters upside down, they seem to lose their stability and fall over or fly apart:

BROCADE-OFFICIAL CITY 錦官城 ("City of Brocade") is a poetic name for Chengdu. It is the name of a section of the city where, centuries before Du's time, there lived an official who regulated the production of silk brocade.

25. *Poem*

River blue—
The birds seem whiter.
Mountains green—
Flowers about to flame.

Spring, I see
Has passed again.
What year will it be
When I go home?

      Du Fu 杜甫
      Tang Dynasty
      About 764 A.D.

1 jyāng (gāng)	江 RIVER	
bì (byak)	碧 BLUE,	
nyău (déu)	鳥 BIRDS	
yú (yū)	逾 MORE	
bái (bak)	白 WHITE	
2 shān (shān)	山 MOUNTAINS	
chīng (tsēng)	青 GREEN,	
hwā (hwā)	花 FLOWERS	
yù (yok)	欲 ABOUT TO	
rán (*nyēn*)	燃 CATCH FIRE	
3 jīn (gīm)	今 NOW	
chwūn (chywīn)	春 SPRING	
kān (kān)	看 SEE	
yòu (yòu)	又 AGAIN	
gwò (gwà)	過 PASSED	

BROKEN LINES 絶句 is the name of a verse-form.

Tang poets used three major verse-forms: *old* verse, *regulated* (or "modern") verse, and *broken lines*.

Old verse is the loosest form. Its only requirements are that lines be the same length (usually either five or seven words) and that every second line rhyme.

Regulated verse poems must be eight lines long, and follow strict tonal and other patterns. They are the Chinese equivalent of sonnets.

Broken lines are like four lines broken from a regulated verse poem. Most of the poems in this book are either broken lines or regulated verse.

The reconstructed Tang pronunciation of this poem is given in parentheses, as it is in poem 18. Du Fu's name was pronounced something like Dò Býo, Li Bai's was Lí Bak.

The tonal patterns followed by regulated verse and broken lines prescribe a balance of *level* tones (marked by a level tone-mark in the Tang pronunciation) and *deflected* tones (all others).

4 hé   何 WHAT
  (hā)
ȑ   日 DAY
  (nyit)
shȑ   是 IS
  (zhì)
gwēi   歸 RETURN
  (gywēi)
nyén   年 YEAR?
  (*nēn*)

The second and fourth words of a line are never of the same tone category. And in each pair of lines, the tones of the second and fourth words follow an *a-b, b-a* pattern that switches to *b-a, a-b* in the next pair of lines.

26. Autumn Meditation

Freezing jade dew
Withers a forest of maples.
At Witch's Mount
And in Witch's Gorge
The air desolately sighs.

Between the walls of the river
Surging waves
Leap to the sky.
Above the mountain barriers
Wind-blown clouds
Meet the earth in darkness.

Clumps of chrysanthemums
Twice now have opened
Tears of other days.
To a solitary boat
Is tied all
My heart's longing for home.

On every side,
Winter clothes
Urge scissors and ruler on.
High in White Emperor City
Wash-blocks beat urgently
At dusk.

Du Fu 杜甫
Tang Dynasty
766 A.D.

秋 *Autumn*
興 *Evoked Thoughts*

1	yù	玉	JADE
	lù	露	DEW
	dyāu	凋	WITHERS-
	shāng	傷	-WOUNDS
	fēng	楓	MAPLE
	shù	樹	TREE
	lín	林	FOREST

2	Wū	巫	WITCH
	Shān	山	MOUNTAIN
	Wū	巫	WITCH
	Syá	峽	GORGE,
	chì	氣	AIR
	syāu	蕭	FORLORN
	sēn	森	DREARY

3	Jyāng	江	RIVER-
	jyēn	間	-SPACE
	bwō	波	TOSSING
	làng	浪	WAVES,
	jyēn	兼	EQUAL TO
	tyen	天	SKY
	yǔng	湧	LEAP UP

4	sāi	塞	BARRIERS-
	shàng	上	-ABOVE
	fēng	風	WIND-
	yún	雲	-CLOUD,
	jyē	接	MEET
	dì	地	GROUND
	yīn	陰	ARE DARK

Du Fu's happy sojourn in Chengdu lasted five years. Then, in 765, his patron died, and he and his family sailed eastward, looking for a new haven (see poem 2).

They found it near White Emperor City (see poem 20), on the gorges of the Yangtze.

In eastern Szechwan province, the Yangtze River flows through more than two hundred miles of treacherous gorges, cutting its way from the Szechwan basin in the west down to the central Chinese lowlands.

WITCH'S GORGE 巫峽 is one of the most desolate and dangerous of the Yangtze gorges. The river passes between high walls of rock that block out the warmth of the sun.

TOSSING WAVES 波浪 is a two-syllable word made up of 波 "waves" and 浪 "tossing waves."

Line 3 swirls up from the river to the sky and line 4 sinks back down again to the ground. The movement of the two lines is like the swirling water and winds of the gorges.

5	tsūng	叢 CLUMPED
	jyú	菊 CHRYSANTHE-MUMS
	lyǎng	兩 TWICE
	kāi	開 HAVE OPENED
	tā	他 OTHER
	r̀	日 DAYS'
	lèi	淚 TEARS
6	gū	孤 SOLITARY
	jōu	舟 BOAT
	yī	一 ONCE (AND FOR ALL)
	jì	繫 IS TIED
	gù	故 OLD
	ywán	園 GARDEN
	syīn	心 HEART
7	hán	寒 COLD
	yī	衣 CLOTHING
	chù	處 PLACE-
	chù	處 -PLACE,
	tswēi	催 URGES ON
	dāu	刀 SCISSORS
	chř	尺 RULER
8	Bái	白 WHITE
	Dì	帝 EMPEROR
	Chéng	城 CITY
	gāu	高 HIGH,
	jí	急 SPEED
	mù	暮 EVENING
	jēn	砧 WASH-BLOCKS

When Du wrote this poem he had been living near the gorges for two years: the chrysanthemums had opened twice.

Du Fu is the acknowledged master of regulated verse. He follows its rules in making lines 3–4 parallel and lines 5–6 parallel, but not doing so with lines 1–2 and 7–8.

Lines 3–4 swirl up and then down. Lines 5–6 open out and then close in again, going from the multiple open chrysanthemums to the single tied heart.

Finally, in the hurry of the last two lines, we have a sense of life rushing on and leaving Du behind.

He never realized his ambition of making great contributions to the welfare of the state. He never even got home to northern China. Four years after writing this poem he died, listlessly wandering the lakes of south central China.

Rough silk cloth cut for winter clothing was softened by being beaten with a wooden mallet on a stone WASH-BLOCK 砧 . Note the element 石 "stone" in this character.

Poems
of War

塞下曲　　　王昌齡

飲馬度秋水水寒風似刀平沙日未沒黯黯
見臨洮昔日長城戰咸言意氣高黃塵足今
古白骨亂蓬蒿

27. The Fortress in Autumn

Last night
The autumn wind
Entered the passes to China.
Northern clouds
And a border moon
Filled the mountains of the west.

Again I urged my flying generals
On in pursuit
Of the haughty barbarians,
Not to let
One horse
Return to the fields of sand.

Marshal YEN WU 嚴武
Tang Dynasty
Possibly 764 A.D.

軍 Army 城 Walled Town   早 Early 秋 Autumn

1 dzwó   昨 YESTERDAY
   yè   夜 NIGHT
   chyōu   秋 AUTUMN
   fēng   風 WIND
   rù   入 ENTERED
   Hàn   漢 CHINA
   gwān   關 PASSES

2 shwò   朔 NORTHERN
   yún   雲 CLOUDS
   byēn   邊 BORDERLAND
   ywè   月 MOON
   mǎn   滿 FILLED
   syī   西 WESTERN
   shān   山 MOUNTAINS

3 gèng   更 AGAIN
   tswēi   催 URGE
   fēi   飛 FLYING
   jyàng   將 GENERALS
   jwēi   追 TO PURSUE
   jyāu   驕 HAUGHTY
   lǔ   虜 CAPTIVES

4 mwò   莫 NOT
   chyěn   遣 SEND AWAY TO
   shā   沙 SAND
   cháng   場 FIELDS
   pǐ   匹 SINGLE

YEN WU (726–765 A.D.) was military governor of Chengdu when Du Fu lived there. He was Du's patron and friend. In 764, his troops defeated an invading force of seventy thousand Tibetan horsemen. He may have written this poem after the battle. A year later he was dead. He is remembered as Du Fu's protector, as a capable general, and as a cruel and rapacious governor.

Chengdu is at the feet of China's WESTERN MOUNTAINS 西山 . Beyond them lies the Tibetan plateau.

Chinese poetry is not all moon and flowers. Especially in Tang times and before, poems about war were common.

CAPTIVES 虜 is a term of abuse that the Tang Chinese used for their Tibetan enemies, the Tu-fan. The year before this poem was written, the Tu-fan had occupied the Chinese capital for a time.

mǎ   馬 HORSE

hwán   還 RETURN

HAUGHTY 驕 *jyau* is made up of 馬 "horse" and the sound-element 喬.

The SAND FIELDS 沙塲 are the deserts of northwestern China, from which many of China's enemies came.

28. Horse Poem

The sand is like snow
In the great desert,
The moon like a hook
Over Mount Yen.

When will my head
Be reined with gold,
And I running swiftly,
Treading clear autumn?

LI HE 李賀
Tang Dynasty
About 810 A.D.

馬 *Horse*
詩 *Poem*

1	dà	大	GREAT
	mwò	漢	DESERT
	shā	沙	SAND
	rú	如	LIKE
	sywě	雪	SNOW

2	Yēn	燕	YEN
	Shān	山	MOUNTAIN
	ywè	月	MOON
	sż	似	RESEMBLES
	gōu	鉤	HOOK

3	hé	何	WHEN
	dāng	當	WILL
	jīn	金	GOLD
	lwò	絡	REIN
	nǎu	腦	BRAIN?

4	kwài	快	SWIFTLY
	dzǒu	走	RUN
	tà	踏	TREAD
	chīng	清	CLEAR
	chyōu	秋	AUTUMN

LI HE (791–817 A.D.) thinks of himself as a fine horse. He is frustrated that his talents have not yet been harnessed in government service. They never were. He died at the age of twenty-six.

To the Tang Chinese, the "fields of sand" north and west of China were both terrifying and romantic. It was from them that the finest horses came.

Every Chinese character is written with a specific number of strokes of the pen, laid down in a specific order:

山 = 丨 山 山
月 = 丿 刀 月 月
如 = 人 女 女 如 如 如

If a character is composed of two or more separate elements, those at the top and left of the character are written first:

沙 = 氵 沙
雪 = 雨 雪
清 = 氵 汁 清

29. Border Song

I water my horse
Crossing an autumn river.
The water is cold,
The wind like a knife.

Away across level sands
The sun is still sinking.
Off in the darkness—
The beginning of the Great Wall.

In former days' battles
By the Great Wall,
Everyone says
Will and spirit ran high.

But yellow earth
Is all that remains,
Then or now.
White bones lie scattered
In the weeds.

WANG CHANG-LING 王昌齡
Tang Dynasty
About 750 A.D.

1	yìn	飲	GIVE DRINK TO
	mǎ	馬	HORSE,
	dù	度	CROSSING
	chyōu	秋	AUTUMN
	shwěi	水	WATER

2	shwěi	水	WATER
	hán	寒	COLD,
	fēng	風	WIND
	sž	似	RESEMBLES
	dāu	刀	KNIFE

3	píng	平	LEVEL
	shǎ	沙	SANDS,
	ř	日	SUN
	wèi	未	NOT YET
	mwò	沒	SUNK

4	àn	黯	DARK
	àn	黯	DARK,
	jyèn	見	SEE
	Lín	臨	LIN
	Táu	洮	TAU

5	syī	昔	PREVIOUS
	ř	日	DAYS
	Cháng	長	LONG
	Chéng	城	WALL
	jàn	戰	BATTLES

In his own time, WANG CHANG-LING (died 756 A.D.) was thought the greatest poet of the age—greater than his contemporaries Li Bai and Du Fu.

This poem has a sturdy, antique air, in part because it imitates a well-known old Han poem:

I water my horse
At a spring by the Great Wall.
The water is cold,
It hurts the horse's bones.

Poets did not shrink from imitating or even quoting the great authors of the past. They thought of this as emulation rather than plagiarism.

LIN-TAU 臨洮 was the place where the Great Wall began, two hundred miles west of the Tang capital. In 714 A.D., during Wang's lifetime, a Chinese army won a great victory there over the Tu-fan Tibetans, killing or capturing several tens of thousands of men.

The LONG WALL 長城 is the Chinese name of what we call

91

6	syén	咸	ALL
	yén	言	SAY
	yì	意	WILL
	chì	氣	SPIRIT
	gāu	高	HIGH

7	hwáng	黃	YELLOW
	chén	塵	DUST
	dzú	足	FILLS
	jīn	今	PRESENT
	gŭ	古	PAST

8	bái	白	WHITE
	gŭ	骨	BONES
	lwàn	亂	LIE DISORDERED
	péng	蓬	BUSHES
	hāu	蒿	

the "Great Wall of China." It was a thousand years old when this poem was written.

SPIRIT 氣 *chì* refers to a person's vitality or "vital-energy." The word's basic meaning is simply "breath."

This poem is a clear example of the standard pattern of development described earlier:

l.1–2 *setting* (cold autumn, going to war),
3–4 *detail* (sunset at Lin-tau),
5–6 *twist* (previous battles),
7–8 *conclusion* (soldiers are now bones).

BUSHES ("weeds") is literally the names of two bushy weeds: TUMBLEWEED 蓬 and WORMWOOD 蒿 .

30. *Wei City Song*

At Wei City
Morning rain
Wets light dust.
Green, green,
By the inn,
The fresh color of the willows.

I urge you
To empty one more
Cup of wine.
For west of the border
You will have no old friends.

WANG WEI 王維
Tang Dynasty
About 750 A.D.

1	Wèi	渭	WEI
	Chéng	城	CITY
	jāu	朝	MORNING
	yǔ	雨	RAIN
	yì	浥	WETS
	chīng	輕	LIGHT
	chén	塵	DUST

2	kè	客	TRAVELERS'
	shè	舍	INN
	chīng	青	GREEN
	chīng	青	GREEN,
	lyǒu	柳	WILLOWS'
	sè	色	COLOR
	syīn	新	NEW

3	chywàn	勸	URGE
	jyūn	君	YOU
	gèng	更	AGAIN
	jìn	盡	EMPTY
	yī	一	ONE
	bēi	杯	CUP
	jyǒu	酒	WINE

4	syī	西	WEST
	chū	出	GO OUT
	Yáng	陽	YANG
	Gwān	關	PASS,
	wú	無	THERE ARE NO
	gù	故	OLD FRIENDS
	rén	人	

Though some poets exalted the lives of the soldiers, the normal attitude to war and to the borderlands was sheer horror. In traditional Chinese culture, nothing could have been worse than to be separated from family and friends.

WEI CITY 渭城 was a town in the western outskirts of the capital, on the road to the borderlands.

The words GREEN GREEN 青青 give the poem a simple, fresh feeling by recalling the opening line of an old poem:

> Green, green,
> The grasses by the river.

This earlier poem is about a wife who longs for her traveling husband.

YANG PASS 陽關 was on the western border of the Tang empire, almost a thousand miles west of the capital.

WANG WEI (701–761 A.D.) was another of Meng Hauran's friends. It was he whom Meng was visiting when they were said to have been surprised by the emperor (see poem 14).

31. *Spring Longing*

When the grasses
Of the north
Are just emerald threads,
The mulberry trees
Of the capital
Hang branches heavy with green.

The days
When you long to return,
Those are the times
When my heart aches.

The spring breeze—
I do not know it.
What business does it have
Coming in through the silk curtains
Round my bed?

LI BAI 李白
Tang Dynasty
About 740 A.D.

春 *Spring*
思 *Longing*

The wife at home longing for her soldier husband is a common figure in Chinese poetry.

The word 思 LONGING basically means "thinking of."

YEN 燕 ("the north") is the area around modern-day Peking. It was in the far northeast of Tang China, and soldiers were stationed there to guard the border.

CHIN 秦 ("the west") is the area around the Tang capital, Chang-an (now Sian), at the western edge of the North China Plain.

LORD 君 ("you") was how friends addressed each other, and how a wife addressed her husband.

SERVANT 妾 ("my") was how wives referred to themselves when speaking to their husbands.

CUT GUTS 斷腸 ("heart aches") is like our "heart-rending" or "heart-broken."

SPRING WIND 春風 is a conventional symbol of sexual feelings.

1	Yēn	燕	YEN
	tsǎu	草	GRASSES
	rú	如	LIKE
	bì	碧	BRIGHT GREEN
	sz̄	絲	THREADS
2	Chín	秦	CHIN
	sāng	桑	MULBERRY TREES
	dī	低	HANG DOWN
	lyù	綠	GREEN
	jř	枝	BRANCHES
3	dāng	當	ON
	jyūn	君	LORD'S
	hwái	懷	CHERISH
	gwēi	歸	RETURN
	ř	日	DAYS
4	shř	是	THESE
	chyè	妾	SERVANT'S
	dwàn	斷	CUT
	cháng	腸	GUTS
	shŕ	時	TIMES
5	chwūn	春	SPRING
	fēng	風	WIND
	bù	不	NOT
	syāng	相	MUTUAL
	shŕ	識	KNOW

6	hé	何	WHAT
	sh̀	事	AFFAIR
	rù	入	ENTER
	lwó	羅	GAUZE SILK
	wéi	帷	CURTAIN?

These last two lines of the poem are reminiscent of the Lady Night Song, poem 7. Li Bai wrote versions of the Lady Night Songs himself, so the resemblance is presumably no accident.

32. *Ballad of the Northwest Frontier*

Sworn
To sweep away the barbarians
And heedless of their own lives,
Five thousand soldiers
In marten-trimmed brocade
Perished in the alien dust.

How sad it is
That bones
By the River of Shifting Sands
Still are men
In spring bedchamber
Dreams.

CHEN TAU 陳陶
Tang Dynasty
Mid 800s A.D.

1	shr̀	誓	SWORN
	său	掃	TO SWEEP
	Syūng	匈	SYUNG
	Nú	奴	NU,
	bù	不	NOT
	gù	顧	REGARD
	shēn	身	SELVES
2	wŭ	五	FIVE
	chyēn	千	THOUSAND
	dyāu	貂	MARTEN
	jĭn	錦	BROCADE,
	sàng	喪	PERISHED
	Hú	胡	NORTHERN BARBARIAN
	chén	塵	DUST
3	kĕ	可	CAN
	lyén	憐	PITY
	Wú	無	NOT
	Dìng	定	FIXED
	Hé	河	RIVER
	byēn	邊	-BESIDE
	gŭ	骨	BONES
4	yóu	猶	STILL
	shr̀	是	ARE
	chwūn	春	SPRING
	gwēi	閨	BEDCHAMBER
	mèng	夢	DREAMS

This eerie poem, although written late in Tang times, is set in the early days of Han, a thousand years before.

LUNG-SYI 隴西 was a district in the northwestern borderlands of the Han empire. The LUNG-SYI BALLAD was a Han song. The SYUNG-NU 匈奴 tribes were the archenemies of the Han Chinese.

The Han soldiers described here are very well equipped. They even have brocade coats lined with marten fur against the cold. At the time, only the Roman empire could rival the wealth and power of Han, just as later only the Muslim empire could rival that of Tang.

CAN PITY 可憐 ("How sad it is") means "pitiable" or "pitiful."

The NOT FIXED RIVER 無定 河 ("River of Shifting Sands") is a major tributary of the Yellow River in China's far north.

SPRING BEDCHAMBER DREAMS 春閨夢 are the amorous dreams of the soldiers' wives.

99

lǐ   裏 -IN

rén   人 MEN

After CHEN TAU (c. 850 A.D.) failed to place in a civil-service examination, he became a student of the Taoist mysteries and a wanderer among China's sacred mountains.

有期不来　　姚月華

銀燭清尊久延佇　出門入門天欲曙月落

星稀竟不来　煙柳朧朧鵶飛去

Poems by
and about
Women

33. "Lady Night" Song of Autumn

She opens her window
To the autumn moon's light.
She puts out the candle
And slips off her silken skirt.

Softly she smiles
Within the curtains of her bed.
She raises her body—
An orchid fragrance spreads.

Anonymous
Six Dynasties Period
300–600 A.D.

1 kāi	開	OPENS
chwāng	窗	WINDOW
chyōu	秋	AUTUMN
ywè	月	MOON
gwāng	光	LIGHT
2 myè	滅	EXTINGUISHES
jú	燭	CANDLE,
jyě	解	TAKES OFF
lwó	羅	GAUZE-SILK
cháng	裳	SKIRT
3 hán	含	HOLDING IN
syàu	笑	SMILE,
wéi	帷	CURTAINS
hwǎng	幌	
lǐ	裏	WITHIN
4 jyǔ	舉	RAISES
tǐ	體	BODY,
lán	蘭	ORCHIDS
hwèi	蕙	
syāng	香	IS FRAGRANT

Chinese poetry shows the same restraint as Chinese painting. Even in such an erotic poem as this one, very little of the body is revealed. Beauty is expressed in clothing and in perfume.

The lines of the poem follow a pattern of classic simplicity:

out to the bright moon (line 1),
in to the darkened room (line 2),
in within the bed-curtains
    (line 3),
out to welcome a lover (line 4).

Such circular *a-b-b-a* patterns (*out-in-in-out*) are common in Chinese literature.

HOLDING IN A SMILE 含笑 really just means "smiling." The word 笑 can mean either "smile" or "laugh." When it is "held in," it is definitely a smile.

The first Lady Night songs were composed and sung by a woman. But Chinese literature is largely a male preserve, and many later ones were written by men.

34. *Jade Stairs Resentment*

On steps of jade
White dew forms.
It creeps within
Her stockings of fine silk
As night grows long.

She lowers then
The water-crystal blind,
And through its glittering gems
She gazes
At the autumn moon.

LI BAI 李白
Tang Dynasty
About 740 A.D.

1	yù	玉	JADE
	jyē	階	STEPS
	shēng	生	IS BORN
	bái	白	WHITE
	lù	露	DEW
2	yè	夜	NIGHT
	jyŏu	久	IS LONG,
	chīn	侵	INVADES
	lwó	羅	GAUZE-SILK
	wà	襪	STOCKINGS
3	chywè	却	THEN
	syà	下	LOWERS
	shwĕi	水	CRYSTAL
	jīng	精	
	lyén	簾	BLINDS
4	líng	玲	GLITTERING
	lúng	瓏	JEWELS,
	wàng	望	GAZES AT
	chyōu	秋	AUTUMN
	ywè	月	MOON

The abandoned sometime favorite of an emperor waits in vain for him to come. When he does not, she retreats into her apartments, lowering the blind.

LI BAI wrote many poems about women, and from a woman's point of view. This is the best known.

Notice the differences among the characters 玉 JADE, 生 IS BORN, and 王 "king."

LOWERS 下 shows the economy and potential ambiguity of Chinese. In different contexts, the word can mean "below" (preposition), "lower" (adjective), "bottom" (noun), or "to lower" (verb).

CRYSTAL 水精 is literally "water-essence."

The word *ling-lung* 玲瓏 GLITTERING JEWELS refers either to the glittering light or the tinkling sound of the crystals strung on the blind.

35. *He Does Not Come*

With silver candles
And clear wine,
Long I have stood here waiting.
Going out the gate
And coming in again
Till nearly first light.

The moon has set,
Stars are few,
Still he does not come.
Wingbeats
In the misty willows—
A magpie takes flight.

The Poetess YAU YWE-HWA 姚月華
     Tang Dynasty (600–900 A.D.)

有 *Have*　　　不 *Does Not*
期 *Appointment*　　來 *Arrive*

1	yín	銀	SILVER
	jú	燭	CANDLES
	chīng	清	CLEAR
	dzwūn	尊	WINE CUPS,
	jyǒu	久	LONG
	yén	延	EXTENDED
	jù	佇	STAND WAIT-ING

2	chū	出	GO OUT
	mén	門	GATE
	rù	入	GO IN
	mén	門	GATE,
	tyēn	天	SKY
	yù	欲	ABOUT TO
	shù	曙	GROW LIGHT

3	ywè	月	MOON
	lwò	落	FALLS
	syīng	星	STARS
	syī	稀	FEW,
	jìng	竟	FINALLY
	bù	不	DOES NOT
	lái	來	COME

YAU YWE-HWA 姚月華 and her father were wanderers on the rivers of eastern China. He was probably a merchant.

Once, when they were living on the Yangtze near Yangjou, she heard a young scholar on a neighboring boat reciting his poems.

She sent her servant to ask for a copy of the poems, and the scholar sent back a beautiful verse expressing his love.

They exchanged a number of poems, but then she and her father moved on, and the young scholar never heard of her again. All he had left were six poems, of which this is one.

STARS 星 *sying* is made up of 日 "sun" and the sound-element 生 *sheng*. In ancient times, when this character was first written, 生 and 星 must

4 yēn	煙	MISTY
lyǒu	柳	WILLOWS
lúng	朧	DRUMBEATS,
túng	瞳	
chywè	鵲	MAGPIE
fēi	飛	FLIES
chyù	去	AWAY

have had the same pronunciation. By the time this poem was written, however, their pronunciations had already drifted apart.

The MAGPIE 鵲 is a large black and white bird like a crow. In China it is associated with happiness. The poetess hears a magpie's wingbeats in the forest, and feels her happiness flying away.

36. The Farewell Feast

How harrowing
A day this is!
The new husband
Faces the old.

I dare not
Either laugh or cry.
Now I know
That human life is hard.

The Princess LE-CHANG　樂昌公主
                    Late Six Dynasties Period
                            About 590 A.D.

餞 *Feast*   自 *Self*
別 *Farewell*   解 *Unburden*

1 jīn   今 THIS
   r̀   日 DAY
   hé   何 HOW
   chyēn   遘 HARROWING!
   tsż   次

2 syīn   新 NEW
   gwān   官 HUSBAND
   dweì   對 FACES
   jyòu   舊 OLD
   gwān   官 HUSBAND

3 syàu   笑 LAUGH
   tí   啼 SOB,
   jyū   俱 BOTH
   bù   不 NOT
   gǎn   敢 DARE

4 fāng   方 ONLY NOW
   syìn   信 BELIEVE
   dzwò   作 TO BE
   rén   人 PERSON
   nán   難 HARD

The Princess LE-CHANG was a sister of the last emperor of the Chen Dynasty, the last of the Six Dynasties.

In 589 A.D., when Chen was conquered by Swei, she was seized from her husband by a member of the new Swei aristocracy.

Some time later he found she still longed for her first husband. He invited the man to a feast and, cruelly, had the princess compose a poem on the occasion. This was her poem.

Eventually, the new husband relented, and allowed her to return to the man she loved.

All the main themes of women's poetry in old China were sad ones: frustration, disappointment, worry, loss. In part this was because of women's dependence on men. In part, it was because men liked to think of women as dependent.

111

37. On Hearing the Lute

Jade fingers
On vermilion strings,
The sound grinding
And then clear.
The ancient grief
Of the Ladies of the River Syang,
So painful to hear.

First it is like the roaring
Of a chill wind.
Then it is the pattering
Of a rain shower at dusk.

Near, it is like a waterfall
Coming down from a green peak.
Far, it is like a black crane
Descending from the blue sky.

Night is deep
When the playing ends.
All I feel is despair.
Beds of orchids
In the moonlit garden
Moist with dew.

Madame MENG, née Swun
孟昌期妻孫氏
Tang Dynasty (600–900 A.D.)

1	yù	玉	JADE
	jř	指	FINGERS
	jū	朱	VERMILION
	syén	絃	STRINGS,
	já	軋	GRINDING
	fù	復	THEN
	chīng	清	CLEAR
2	Syāng	湘	SYANG RIVER
	Fēi	妃	CONSORTS
	chóu	惆	DESPAIR
	ywàn	怨	HURT
	dzwèi	最	MOST
	nán	難	DIFFICULT TO
	tīng	聽	LISTEN TO
3	chū	初	FIRST
	yí	疑	SUSPECT IS
	sà	颯	BLUSTERING
	sà	颯	
	lyáng	涼	COOL
	fēng	風	WIND
	jìng	勁	STRONG
4	yòu	又	AGAIN
	sž	似	RESEMBLES
	syāu	蕭	PATTERING
	syāu	蕭	
	mù	暮	EVENING
	yǔ	雨	RAIN
	líng	零	SHOWERING

The 琴 *chin* is not really a
LUTE. It is more like a long,
narrow zither or dulcimer. But
its music is like that of the lute
or the harp. It has seven
strings and is laid flat and
plucked. The Japanese *koto* is
its descendant.

The SYANG RIVER CONSORTS
湘妃 ("Ladies of the River
Syang") were the two daugh-
ters of the mythical emperor
Yu, and consorts of his succes-
sor Shwun. When their hus-
band died, they are said to
have drowned themselves in
the River Syang. They were
worshiped as goddesses in
southern China.

Madame MENG was the wife
of a scholar-official, and used
to do much of his writing for
him. One day, however, she
suddenly said, "Intellectual
creation is not something for a
woman," and burned every-
thing she had written. Only
two of her poems survive.

The element 雨 RAIN forms
part of many characters having
to do with precipitation—for
example:

113

5	jìn	近	NEAR
	bǐ	比	COMPARES WITH
	lyóu	流	FLOWING
	chywán	泉	SPRING
	lái	來	COMING FROM
	bì	碧	GREEN
	jàng	嶂	PEAK
6	ywǎn	遠	FAR
	rú	如	IS LIKE
	sywán	玄	BLACK
	hè	鶴	CRANE
	syà	下	DESCENDING FROM
	chīng	青	BLUE
	míng	冥	HIGH SKY
7	yè	夜	NIGHT
	shēn	深	DEEP,
	tán	彈	PLAYING
	bà	罷	ENDS,
	kān	堪	ENDURE
	chóu	惆	DESPAIR
	chàng	悵	
8	lù	露	DEW
	shī	濕	MOISTENS
	tsūng	叢	CLUSTERED
	lán	蘭	ORCHIDS,
	ywè	月	MOON
	mǎn	滿	FILLS
	tíng	庭	COURTYARD

雪 "snow"　　露 "dew"
電 "lightning"　霽 "clearing up"

The ancient form of 雨 clearly shows raindrops falling from the sky: 门 .

The word SPRING 泉 is used for any small stream. The element 水 is the character for "water."

There is more than one word that can be translated PEAK. The word 嶂 *jang* emphasizes the screening aspect of a peak. The word 峯 *feng* suggests one that stabs the sky like a lance. Both words contain the element 山 "mountain."

The CRANE 鶴 is a magical bird in China. It is associated with long life and Taoist sorcery.

The word 彈 PLAYING contains the element 弓 "bow." Plucking a stringed instrument is like drawing the string of a bow.

Music played one evening over a thousand years ago becomes vividly present in this poem.

Madame Meng was a minor poet. It is only by the merest chance that any of her work has survived. Yet I find this poem at least as moving as the next, one by the great Li Bai about another musical evening.

38. *Hearing a Monk of Shu Play the Lute*

The monk of Shu,
Bearing his lute "Green Damask,"
Descends in the west
The peak E-mei.

The moment his hands
Begin to play across the strings,
It is like hearing the wind
In the pines of ten thousand valleys.

The traveler's mind
Is washed in flowing water.
Lingering echoes
Sound in the frost-ringing bells.

Unnoticed,
Evening has come
To green mountains.
The clouds of autumn—
How many layers dark?

LI BAI 李白
Tang Dynasty
About 725 A.D.

1 Shǔ	蜀	SHU
sēng	僧	MONK
bàu	抱	HOLDING
Lyù	綠	"GREEN
Chǐ	綺	DAMASK"
2 syī	西	WEST
syà	下	DESCENDS
É	峨	E
Méi	嵋	MEI
fēng	峯	PEAK
3 wèi	爲	FOR
wǒ	我	ME
yī	一	ONCE
hwēi	揮	WAVES
shǒu	手	HANDS
4 rú	如	LIKE
tīng	聽	HEARING
wàn	萬	TEN THOU- SAND
hwò	壑	VALLEYS
sūng	松	PINES
5 kè	客	TRAVELER'S
syīn	心	MIND
syǐ	洗	WASHED
lyóu	流	FLOWING
shwěi	水	WATER

SHU 蜀 is the ancient name of the rich western province of Szechwan.

YU 潀 is the monk's religious name. It means "deep," as in "deep wisdom."

GREEN DAMASK 綠綺 was the name of a famous ancient lute. The monk's lute was not really called "Green Damask"; Li Bai just wants to suggest that it is a fine one. The effect is something like calling a violin a "Stradivarius."

E-MEI 峨嵋 is a particularly beautiful mountain in Szechwan. Many Buddhist monasteries were established there. Notice the mountains 山 in the two characters.

The 扌 in 揮 WAVES is a form of 手 HAND.

The 耳 in 聽 HEARING is an ear.

The word 心 MIND literally means "heart." The Chinese, like most other peoples, used to believe that the mind was centered in the heart.

The FROST BELLS 霜鐘 ("frost-ringing bells") were an

6	yú	餘	LEFTOVER
	syǎng	響	ECHOES
	rù	入	ENTER
	shwāng	霜	FROST
	jūng	鍾	BELLS
7	bù	不	NOT
	jywé	覺	NOTICE
	bì	碧	GREEN
	shān	山	MOUNTAIN
	mù	暮	EVENING
8	chyōu	秋	AUTUMN
	yún	雲	CLOUDS
	àn	暗	DARK
	jī	幾	HOW MANY
	chúng	重	TIMES?

ancient set of bells so fine that they would ring when frost fell. Here, the expression is an elegant overstatement.

The names of Chinese colors are difficult to translate. The color 碧 GREEN, for example, is the color of green jasper, of luxuriant vegetation, and of the clear sky. I have translated it elsewhere as "blue," "blue-green," "emerald," and "jasper green."

39. Lyrics to the Tune "Tipsy in the Flowers' Shade"

Thin mist.
Thick clouds.
Sad eternal day.
Incense crystals melt away
In a censer
Like an animal of gold.

The Fair Season once again
Of the Autumn Festival.
Deep in the night
The cold first reached
The jade pillow and silken curtains
Of my bed.

It is dusk.
I drink wine
By the eastern fence.
A hidden fragrance fills my sleeves.

Oh, do not say
My spirit is not worn—
As curtains furl
In the west wind,
I am more withered
Than the chrysanthemums'
Yellow flowers.

The Poetess LI CHING-JAU 李清照
Southern Sung period
About 1125 A.D.

醉 "Tipsy   陰 Shade"
花 Flowers'   詞 Lyrics

1	báu	薄	THIN
	wù	霧	MIST
	núng	濃	THICK
	yún	雲	CLOUDS,
	chóu	愁	SORROWFUL
	yūng	永	ETERNAL
	jòu	晝	DAYTIME
2	rwèi	瑞	BORNEOL
	nǎu	腦	INCENSE
	syāu	消	MELTS AWAY
	jīn	金	GOLDEN
	shòu	獸	ANIMAL
3	jyā	佳	FINE
	jyé	節	SEASON
	yòu	又	AGAIN
	Chúng	重	AUTUMN
	Yáng	陽	FESTIVAL
4	yù	玉	JADE
	jěn	枕	PILLOW
	shā	紗	THIN SILK
	shú	幬	CURTAINS
5	bàn	半	HALF
	yè	夜	NIGHT
	lyáng	涼	COOL
	chū	初	FIRST
	tòu	透	PENETRATES

LI CHING-JAU (born 1084 A.D.) was China's greatest woman poet. She was one of few women in old China whose family thought it advisable or worthwhile to give a good education.

She and her husband were well-known antiquarians and together wrote a major catalog of art objects.

BORNEOL INCENSE 瑞腦 ("incense crystals") is a mild camphor-like flake crystal incense. Its name 瑞腦 means "auspicious brain." It is also called "auspicious dragon brain" and "ice flakes."

AUTUMN FESTIVAL 重陽 was on the ninth day of the ninth month of the old Chinese year—mid to late October by our calendar. The custom was to climb to a high place, drink wine, and compose poems.

Notice the element 木 "wood" in the word 枕 PILLOW. Traditional Chinese pillows are small wooden or ceramic objects. This JADE PILLOW 玉枕 may have been

6 dūng	東	EASTERN
lí	籬	BAMBOO FENCE
bǎ	把	HOLD
jyǒu	酒	WINE,
hwáng	黃	YELLOW
hwūn	昏	DUSK
hòu	後	AFTER
7 yǒu	有	THERE IS
àn	暗	HIDDEN
syāng	香	FRAGRANCE
yíng	盈	FILLS
syòu	袖	SLEEVES
8 mwò	莫	DO NOT
dàu	道	SAY
bù	不	NOT
syāu	銷	MELT DOWN
hwún	魂	SPIRIT
9 lyén	簾	CURTAINS
jywǎn	捲	FURL
syī	西	WEST
fēng	風	WIND
10 rén	人	PERSON
bǐ	比	COMPARED TO
hwáng	黃	CHRYSAN-
hwā	花	THEMUMS
shòu	瘦	EMACIATED

made of wood inlaid with semi-precious stones.

Li Ching-jau wrote a kind of poetry called 詞 *tsz* or "song-lyrics." These were lyrics written to a number of standard popular tunes. Lines tend to be of unequal lengths and rhyme-schemes irregular. The form originated during Tang but reached its peak during Sung.

Li wrote this one while her husband was away from home and sent it to him in a letter. He thought he could do better and spent three days and nights writing fifteen lyrics of his own. When he showed all sixteen to a friend, the friend unerringly chose the last three lines of this poem as the best of the lot.

CHRYSANTHEMUMS 黃花 is literally "yellow flowers." This is the common name for chrysanthemums. The literary name is 菊 *jyu*. Song-lyrics use the language of everyday speech rather than that of high literature.

40. *Lyrics to the Tune "Spring in Wu-ling"*

The wind is still,
The earth smells sweet—
The flowers all have fallen.
As evening comes
I tiredly comb my hair.

His things remain
But he is gone—
Everything is over.
When I try to speak
Up well the tears.

I hear it said that spring's
Still at its height
At Double Creek.
I think of going to sail
The light boats there.

But I fear
The "grasshopper boats"
At Double Creek
Could never move
So great a load
Of sorrow.

The Poetess Li CHING-JAU　李清照
　　　　Southern Sung period
　　　　　1135 A.D.

1	fēng	風	WIND
	jù	住	STOPS,
	chén	塵	DUST
	syāng	香	FRAGRANT,
	hwā	花	FLOWERS
	yǐ	已	HAVE
	jìn	盡	ALL FINISHED
2	r̀	日	DAY
	wǎn	晚	AT EVENING,
	jywàn	倦	TIRED
	shū	梳	COMB
	tóu	頭	HEAD
3	wù	物	THINGS
	shr̀	是	YES,
	rén	人	PERSON
	fēi	非	NO,
	shr̀	事	
	shr̀	事	EVERYTHING
	syōu	休	HAS ENDED
4	yù	欲	WANT TO
	yǔ	語	SPEAK,
	lèi	淚	TEARS
	syēn	先	FIRST
	lyóu	流	FLOW
5	wén	聞	HEAR
	shwō	說	SAID
	Shwāng	雙	DOUBLE
	Syī	溪	CREEK

LI CHING-JAU and her husband were famous lovers. Their life together was a model of harmonious affection. Her grief at his early death—when they were both forty-six—produced some of China's most moving poems. This one was written in 1135, six years after he died.

WU-LING 武陵 is an area of south central China, but "Spring in Wu-ling" is just the name of the tune to which Li wrote these lyrics.

EVERYTHING 事事 is literally "thing-thing." In Chinese there are two words for "thing": 物 *wu* for objects and 事 *shr* for events.

Li and her husband originally lived in northern China. But in 1127 they fled south before the invading Golden Tartars, who seized the north from the Sung Dynasty.

Two years later, on his way to a new government posting in the semitropical south, Li's husband fell ill with dysentery and malaria. She rushed to his side just in time to watch him die. She spent the last twenty

chwūn	春	SPRING
shàng	尚	STILL
hău	好	LOVELY

6	yě	也	AND
	nǐ	擬	PLAN TO
	fàn	汎	SAIL
	chīng	輕	LIGHT
	jōu	舟	BOATS

7	jǐ	只	ONLY
	kǔng	恐	FEAR
	Shwāng	雙	DOUBLE
	Syī	溪	CREEK
	dzé	舴	TINY
	měng	艋	
	jōu	舟	BOATS

8	dzài	載	CARRY
	bù	不	NOT
	dùng	動	MOVE
	syǔ	許	VERY
	dwō	多	MUCH
	chóu	愁	SORROW

years of her life keeping her love for him alive in her poetry.

Their love is said to have been fated. The story goes that as a young boy, Li's husband dreamed of a strange book. When he awoke, all he could remember were four Chinese characters, which he did not then recognize:

1: 言 "speak" and 司 "officer" combined as one character.
2: The character 安 "peace" with its upper part removed.
3 and 4: 芝 "orchid" and 芙 "hibiscus" stripped of their grasses (艹).

His father interpreted this to mean that he would become "the husband of a song-lyric poetess:"

1: 言 + 司 = 詞 *"song-lyric"*
2: 安 − 宀 = 女 *"woman"*
3: 芝 − 艹 = 之 *"'s"*
4: 芙 − 艹 = 夫 *"husband"*

DOUBLE CREEK 雙溪 is near where Li spent the last twenty years of her life, living with her brother and his family.

The phrase 舴艋舟 TINY BOAT ("grasshopper boat") is closely related to the word 蚱蜢 "grasshopper." The element 舟 means "boat." The element 虫 means "insect."

41. Lyrics to the Tune "Fairy Grotto"

Skin of ice.
Bones of jade.
Always cool and unperspiring.

To the palace by the water
Comes a breeze,
Filling it with hidden fragrance.

Embroidered curtains open.
A ray of moonlight
Peeks in at her.
She is not yet asleep,
But leans against the pillow,
Hairpin awry
And hair tousled.

She rises.
I take her white hand.
In all the doors and courtyards
There is silence.

From time to time
A shooting star
Crosses the Milky Way.

I ask how late it is:
Already midnight.
Golden waves of moonlight fade,
The stars of the Jeweled Cord
Roll low.

On my fingers I count the time
Until the west wind comes again,
Saying nothing of the flowing years
That steal away in darkness.

Su Shr 蘇軾
Sung Dynasty
1082 A.D.

1	bīng	冰	ICE
	jī	肌	FLESH
	yù	玉	JADE
	gŭ	骨	BONES
2	dż	自	OF THEM-SELVES
	chīng	清	PURE
	lyáng	涼	COOL,
	wú	無	WITHOUT
	hàn	汗	PERSPIRATION
3	shwěi	水	WATER
	dyèn	殿	PALACE
	fēng	風	WIND
	lái	來	COMES,
	àn	暗	HIDDEN
	syāng	香	FRAGRANCE
	mǎn	滿	FILLS
4	syòu	繡	EMBROIDERED
	lyén	簾	CURTAINS
	kāi	開	OPEN
5	yī	一	ONE
	dyěn	點	BIT OF
	míng	明	BRIGHT
	ywè	月	MOON
	kwēi	窺	PEEKS AT
	rén	人	PERSON

The poetess Li Ching-jau was among the greatest lyric poets, but more lyrics were written *about* women than *by* them. Many of these are mildly erotic, with a magical, sweet, sparkling beauty.

The word 仙 FAIRY refers to those who have refined themselves by diet, exercise, and meditation to the point that they are almost immortal. Such "immortals" live hidden in the mountains, sometimes in caves, and can ride the clouds and command cranes and dragons to carry them.

In his preface to this poem Su Shr wrote:

"When I was seven years old I met an old nun from Mt. E-mei. Her surname was Ju. I don't remember her given name. She was ninety, and said she used to go with her teacher to the palace of Meng Chang, Lord of Shu ('emperor' of the short-lived Shu Dynasty, which held Szechwan from 934 until it was crushed by the Sung in 965).

6	rén	人	PERSON
	wèi	未	NOT YET
	chǐn	寢	SLEEPING
7	yǐ	敧	LEANS ACROSS
	jěn	枕	PILLOW,
	chāi	釵	HAIRPIN
	héng	橫	SIDEWAYS,
	bìn	鬢	HAIR AT TEMPLES
	lwàn	亂	DISORDERED
8	chǐ	起	ARISE
	lái	來	
	syé	攜	HOLD
	sù	素	WHITE
	shǒu	手	HAND
9	tíng	庭	COURTYARDS
	hù	戶	DOORS
	wú	無	THERE IS NO
	shēng	聲	SOUND
10	shŕ	時	TIME
	jyèn	見	SEE
	lyóu	流	FLOWING
	syīng	星	STAR
	dù	渡	CROSS
	Hé	河	MILKY WAY
	Hàn	漢	
11	shŕ	試	TEST
	wèn	問	ASK
	yè	夜	NIGHT
	rú	如	HOW LATE?
	hé	何	

"Once, when it was very warm, the lord and his concubine Lady Flower-Stamen were taking the cool of the night by the Great Pool. He composed a poem there, and the old nun remembered every word of it.

"But forty years have passed since I met her. She is long dead and all I can remember are the poem's first two lines. One day when I was thinking about them I suddenly realized they were written to the tune 'Fairy Grotto.' So I went ahead and completed the poem with words of my own."

ARISE 起來 is literally "rise-come." Exactly these same words are still used in modern spoken Chinese. Literary Chinese would just be 起 RISE.

The pale WHITE 素 skin of a lady who has leisure to avoid the sun was considered beautiful in China as in the West.

This large palace has many separate COURTYARDS 庭 .

The MILKY WAY 河漢 has several names in Chinese. Here it is named after two of China's great rivers, the Yellow River (He 河) and the Han 漢 . It is also called the "River of Heaven" or the "Silver River."

The THIRD WATCH 三更 is the period from about 11 P.M. to 1 A.M.

127

12	yè	夜	NIGHT
	yǐ	巳	ALREADY
	sān	三	THIRD
	gēng	更	WATCH
13	jīn	金	GOLDEN
	bwō	波	WAVES
	dàn	淡	PALE
14	Yù	玉	JADE
	Shéng	繩	CORD
	dī	低	LOW
	jwǎn	轉	ROLLS
15	dàn	但	ONLY
	chyū	屈	CROOK
	jř	指	FINGERS
	syī	西	WEST
	fēng	風	WIND
	jǐ	幾	WHAT
	shř	時	TIME
	lái	來	COME?
16	yòu	又	ALSO
	bù	不	NOT
	dàu	道	SPEAK OF
	lyóu	流	FLOWING
	nyén	年	YEARS
17	àn	暗	DARKNESS
	jūng	中	-WITHIN
	tōu	偷	STEAL
	hwàn	換	EXCHANGE

GOLDEN WAVES 金波 is a standard poetic expression for moonlight.

PALE 淡 literally means "bland." Notice the element 氵 "water." The word was originally used for bland food or drink.

The JADE CORD 玉繩 ("Jeweled Cord") consists of two small stars in our constellation Draco, between the handle of the Big Dipper and the North Star. To us, jade is a semiprecious stone. In Chinese culture it is *the* jewel par excellence.

When the Chinese count on their hands, they CROOK 屈 their FINGERS 指 one at a time, beginning with the thumb. At six, they start spreading their fingers again, again beginning with the thumb. This makes it possible to count to ten on each hand.

The WEST WIND 西風 is the cool wind of autumn, the coming of which will mean that another summer has passed.

SU SHR writes as if he were the Lord of Shu, walking out in his palace with his favorite concubine on a summer night. But he knows that both lord and concubine are long dead—the flowing years have stolen away, replacing each other one by one.

42. The Temporary Palace

Desolate and forlorn,
The old temporary palace.
The palace flowers
Lonely red.

White-haired palace ladies
Still sit there,
Talking of an emperor
Long dead.

YWAN JEN 元 稹
Tang Dynasty
About 800 A.D.

1 lyáu   家 LONELY
   lwò   落 DESOLATE
   gŭ   古 OLD
   syíng   行 TRAVELING
   gūng   宮 PALACE

2 gūng   宮 PALACE
   hwā   花 FLOWERS
   jì   寂 LONELY
   mwò   寞
   húng   紅 RED

3 bái   白 WHITE
   tóu   頭 HEAD
   gūng   宮 PALACE
   nyŭ   女 WOMEN
   dzài   在 ARE THERE

4 syén   閒 AT EASE
   dzwò   坐 SIT
   shwō   説 SPEAKING OF
   Sywán   玄 SYWAN
   Dzūng   宗 DZUNG

A TRAVELING PALACE 行宮 ("Temporary Palace") was an auxiliary palace outside the capital, something like Camp David or Sandringham.

The emperor SYWAN-DZUNG 玄宗 ("an emperor long dead") presided over the golden age of Tang. His love affair with the concubine Yang Gwei-fei is the most famous in all of Chinese history.

It was also the beginning of the dynasty's decline, however. The honors he showered on Yang's relatives provoked a powerful military commander into rebellion.

In 756, rebels took the capital. The emperor and his court were forced to flee over the mountains into Szechwan. The imperial guard blamed Yang for the disaster. In mid-flight, deep among the mountains, it forced the emperor to have her strangled with a silken cord.

43. *Hearing Jang Li-ben's Daughter Sing*

Towering hat
And broad sleeves,
She is dressed in the fashion
Of the palaces of the south.
She walks alone
In a quiet courtyard,
Seeking the cool of the night.

Taking her hairpin of jade
She beats the measure
On the trunk of a bamboo tree
By the steps.
High and clear she sings—
The moon like frost.

> Attributed to GAU SHR　高適
> Tang Dynasty
> About 750 A.D.

聽 *Hear* 本 *-ben*
張 *Jang* 女 *Daughter*
立 *Li-* 吟 *Sing*

1 wēi	危	TOWERING
gwān	冠	HEADDRESS
gwǎng	廣	BROAD
syòu	袖	SLEEVES,
Chǔ	楚	CHU
gūng	宮	PALACE
jwāng	妝	BEDECKED
2 dú	獨	ALONE
bù	步	PACES
syén	閑	QUIET
tíng	庭	COURTYARD,
jú	逐	PURSUING
yè	夜	NIGHT
lyáng	涼	COOLNESS
3 dž	自	SELF
bǎ	把	TAKES
yù	玉	JADE
chāi	釵	HAIRPIN,
chyāu	敲	TAPS
chì	砌	STEPS
jú	竹	BAMBOO

A strange story is associated with this poem.

The daughter of a minor official called JANG LI-BEN was possessed by a spirit. She had never learned to read, but when the spirit came upon her she would dress in fine clothes and chant poems in her room. This was one of the poems she chanted. As soon as the spirit left her, she would break down in wild weeping and crying.

She was cured by two small pills given to her father by a Buddhist priest. Afterward she said she had been possessed by a fox-spirit that lived among the bamboos at the nearby grave of the well-known poet GAU SHR.

The Tang Chinese believed that some foxes were actually

4	chīng	清	CLEAR
	gē	歌	SINGS
	yī	一	ONE
	chyǔ	曲	SONG,
	ywè	月	MOON
	rú	如	LIKE
	shwāng	霜	FROST

spirits who craved intercourse with human beings, and could assume human shape.

Despite its strange origin, this poem is traditionally included among Gau Shr's works.

The CHU PALACE 楚宮 style of women's clothing originated in the ancient southern kingdom of Chu. It included close-fitting dresses that were rather old-fashioned by the time this poem was written.

CLEAR 清 here means "unaccompanied."

夜雨　　白居易

早蛩啼復歇殘燈滅又明隔牕知夜雨

芭蕉先有聲

Landscape/ Enlightenment

44. *An Invitation to My Friend Lyou*

"Green Ant"
New wine.
Red clay
Little warming-stove.

It is late
And about to snow.
Could you drink
A cup with me?

BAI JYU-YI 白居易
Tang Dynasty
817 A.D.

1	lyù	綠	GREEN
	yǐ	螘	ANT
	syīn	新	NEW
	pēi	醅	UNFILTERED
	jyǒu	酒	WINE
2	húng	紅	RED
	ní	泥	CLAY
	syǎu	小	LITTLE
	hwǒ	火	FIRE-
	lú	爐	-STOVE
3	wǎn	晚	EVENING
	lái	來	COMES,
	tyēn	天	SKY
	yù	欲	ABOUT TO
	sywě	雪	SNOW
4	néng	能	CAN
	yǐn	飲	DRINK
	yī	一	ONE
	bēi	杯	CUP
	wú	無	OR NOT?

LYOU NINETEEN 劉十九 ("my friend Lyou") was evidently the nineteenth-oldest child of his generation in the Lyou family. NINETEEN is literally "ten-nine" 十九 .

The GREEN ANTS 綠螘 were flecks of greenish-white scum on the surface of newly fermented rice wine.

UNFILTERED WINE 醅酒 was cheap, raw wine that had not yet been filtered clear. The 酉 in these characters means "wine."

The FIRE-STOVE 火爐 ("warming-stove") was for heating the wine. Like Japanese *sake*, Chinese wines were and are often heated before drinking. Chinese "wines" range in alcohol content from 4% (about equal to beer) to 40% (about equal to whisky). Some of the more popular varieties are made from rice, millet, sorghum, or beans. Grape wine was imported into Tang China from Central Asia as an exotic delicacy.

45. *Roaming Chyen-tang Lake in Spring*

North
Of Lone Mountain Temple,
West
Of the Pavilion of Duke Jya,
The water's surface
Is stilled
By the clouds' feet
Of rain.

Here and there
Early warblers
Squabble in warm trees.
By someone's house
New swallows
Take beakfuls of spring mud.

Scattered flowers
Slowly grow
To dazzle a man's eyes.
Shallow grasses
Just enough
To drown the horse's hooves.

I most love
This east side of the lake.
I cannot wander here enough:
In the shade of green willows
An embankment of white sand.

BAI JYU-YI 白居易
Tang Dynasty
823 A.D.

錢	*Chyen-*	春 *Spring*
塘	*-tang*	行 *Journey*
湖	*Lake*	

1	Gū	孤	SOLITARY
	Shān	山	MOUNTAIN
	Sż	寺	TEMPLE
	běi	北	NORTH,
	Jyǎ	賈	JYA
	Tíng	亭	PAVILION
	syī	西	WEST
2	shwěi	水	WATER
	myèn	面	SURFACE
	chū	初	FIRST
	píng	平	BECOMES LEVEL,
	yún	雲	CLOUD
	jyǎu	脚	FEET
	dī	低	BENEATH
3	jǐ	幾	SEVERAL
	chù	處	PLACES
	dzǎu	早	EARLY
	yīng	鶯	WARBLERS
	jēng	爭	SQUABBLE
	nwǎn	暖	WARM
	shù	樹	TREES
4	shwéi	誰	SOMEONE'S
	jyā	家	HOUSE
	syīn	新	NEW
	yèn	燕	SWALLOWS
	jwó	啄	PECK

CHYEN-TANG LAKE 錢塘湖 is another name for the famous West Lake at Hangchow, the most beautiful lake in China.

SOLITARY MOUNTAIN TEMPLE 孤山寺 stood on an island called Solitary Mountain 孤山.

JYA PAVILION 賈亭 ("the pavilion of Duke Jya") was a small pavilion built twenty-five years earlier by Jya Chywan, then governor of Hangchow.

CLOUD FEET 雲脚 are showers falling from clouds passing across the lake on this warm spring day. The clouds seem to still the surface of the water with their feet of rain.

BAI JYU-YI was the newly appointed governor of Hangchow. He had just made the long journey down from the capital the previous autumn. The warmth and beauty of spring in the southeast enthralled him.

SWALLOWS 燕 swoop down and take beakfuls of mud for their nests. In Chinese as in

| chwūn | 春 | SPRING |
| ní | 泥 | MUD |

5 lwàn	亂	DISORDERED
hwā	花	FLOWERS
jyèn	漸	GRADUALLY
yù	欲	ABOUT TO
mí	迷	CONFUSE
rén	人	PERSON'S
yěn	眼	EYES

6 chyěn	淺	SHALLOW
tsǎu	草	GRASSES
tsái	纔	BARELY
néng	能	ABLE TO
mwò	沒	SUBMERGE
mǎ	馬	HORSE'S
tí	蹄	HOOVES

7 dzwèi	最	MOST
aì	愛	LOVE
hú	湖	LAKE
dūng	東	EAST,
sying	行	TRAVEL
bù	不	NOT
dzú	足	ENOUGH

8 lyù	綠	GREEN
yáng	楊	WILLOWS
yīn	陰	SHADE
lǐ	裏	WITHIN,
bái	白	WHITE
shā	沙	SAND
dī	堤	EMBANKMENT

English, the words "swallow" (燕 yen) and "to swallow" (嚥 yen) are closely related.

The character for HOUSE 家 is made up of a pig 豕 beneath a roof 宀.

FLOWERS 花 hwa is made up of 艹 "plant" and 化 the sound hwa. Though 化 means "transform," here it is probably used only for its sound.

Notice how similar 眼 EYES is to 眠 "sleep."

In ancient times, the character for HORSE was clearly a schematic drawing of a horse: 𢒠 . This evolved to 𢒠 and then, around 200 B.C., to the modern form 馬 .

The West Lake at Hangchow is today the most beloved scenic place in China. Much of its gentle scenery is man made— islands, embankments, the contours of the lake itself.

Though the lake is much altered, the WHITE SAND EMBANKMENT 白沙堤 remains. It is an earthen dike or causeway that cuts across the northern part of the lake.

Today the embankment is called "Bai's Embankment" 白堤 , in honor of the poet, whose surname 白 means "white."

46. Moored on the Chin-hwai River

Mist veils cold water,
Moonlight veils the sand.
Moored at night
On the Chin-hwai River
Near a wine-shop.

The singing-girl
Does not know the bitterness
Of a nation ruined.
Across the river
She still sings
"Flower of the Inner Court."

Du Mu 杜牧
Tang Dynasty
About 830 A.D.

泊 *Moored*
秦 *Chin-*
淮 *-hwai*

1 yēn	煙	SMOKE
lúng	籠	BASKETS
hán	寒	COLD
shwěi	水	WATER,
ywè	月	MOON
lúng	籠	BASKETS
shā	沙	SAND
2 yè	夜	NIGHT
bwó	泊	MOORED
Chín	秦	CHIN
Hwái	淮	HWAI,
jìn	近	NEAR
jyǒu	酒	WINE
jyā	家	HOUSE
3 shāng	商	MERCHANT'S
nyǔ	女	DAUGHTER
bù	不	DOES NOT
jr̄	知	KNOW
wáng	亡	PERISHED
gwó	國	NATION
hèn	恨	BITTER
		REGRET
4 gé	隔	ACROSS
jyāng	江	RIVER

The CHIN-HWAI 秦淮 River enters the Yangtze at the great southern city now called Nanking ("Southern Capital"), but in Tang times called Jinling ("Golden Hill").

SMOKE 煙 is a poetic way of saying "mist."

BASKETS 籠 means "holds in a basket." A 籠 is a shallow wicker basket. The element 竹 means "bamboo." The element 龍 is pronounced *lung*. It is also the word for "dragon," but this has nothing whatsoever to do with its use here.

Du Mu came from a distinguished noble family. Frustrated by the weakness of the late Tang court, he let his own official career take second place to a life of pleasure.

MERCHANT'S DAUGHTER 商女 was contemporary slang for "singing-girl." In fact, many singing-girls were the daughters of merchants.

yóu 猶 STILL
chàng 唱 SINGS
Hòu 後 "BACK
Tíng 庭 COURTYARD
Hwā 花 FLOWER"

BACK COURTYARD FLOWER 後
庭花 ("Flower of the Inner
Court") is a song in praise of
the beauty of a lady of the
court. It was written around
585 A.D. by the pleasure-loving
last emperor of the Chen
Dynasty (see poem 36). When
invading forces entered his
palace, they found him hiding
in a well with his favorite
concubines.

47. *Night Mooring at Maple Bridge*

Moon sets.
Crows caw.
Frost fills the air.
Maple trees by the river
And the lamps of fishermen
I face
In a sorrowful drowse.

From Cold Mountain Monastery,
Beyond the old city-wall,
Reaching the traveler's boat
Comes the sound
Of the midnight bell.

> JANG JI 張繼
> Tang Dynasty
> About 750 A.D.

1 ywè　月 MOON
lwò　落 FALLS,
wū　烏 CROWS
tí　啼 CAW,
shwāng　霜 FROST
mǎn　滿 FILLS
tyēn　天 SKY

2 jyāng　江 RIVER
fēng　楓 MAPLES,
yú　漁 FISHERMEN'S
hwǒ　火 FIRES,
dwèi　對 FACING
chóu　愁 SORROWFULLY
myén　眠 DROWSE

3 Gū　姑 GU
Sū　蘇 SU
chéng　城 CITY WALL
wài　外 OUTSIDE,
Hán　寒 COLD
Shān　山 MOUNTAIN
Sż　寺 TEMPLE

4 yè　夜 NIGHT-
bàn　半 -MID
jūng　鐘 BELL
shēng　聲 SOUND
dàu　到 REACHES

Chinese poets return to the same themes and situations again and again. This can sometimes be tiresome. But good poets can make the same situations seem completely fresh and new. This poem and the previous one are examples.

MAPLE BRIDGE 楓橋 is in the western suburbs of the modern garden city of Soochow. Both 楓 MAPLE and 橋 BRIDGE contain the element 木 "wood."

See how similar 烏 CROW is to 鳥 BIRD.

FISHERMEN'S FIRES 漁火 are the lanterns hung on fishing boats in southern China to attract fish at night.

GU-SU 姑蘇 is an old name for Soochow.

COLD MOUNTAIN TEMPLE 寒山寺 is situated near Maple Bridge. It is said to have gained its name from the legend that the crazy poet-monk Han Shan ("Cold Mountain") once lived there.

kè 客 TRAVELER'S
chwán 船 BOAT

Few Chinese temples rang a MIDNIGHT BELL 夜半鐘 . One Chinese commentator criticizes the poet for inventing the whole idea. Other commentators go to great lengths to prove that temples around Soochow did in fact ring a bell at midnight.

48. Visiting the Temple
of Accumulated Fragrance

Not knowing the way
To the temple,
I enter several miles
Into cloudy peaks.

Ancient trees,
A deserted path—
Deep in the mountains
Somewhere a bell.

The sound of a spring
Choked by towering rocks.
The color of sunlight
Chilled by green pines.

Near evening
At the corner of an empty pool,
Calm meditation
Subdues poison dragons
Of the mind.

WANG WEI 王維
Tang Dynasty
About 750 A.D.

過 *Visiting* 積 *-Accumulated*
香 *Fragrance-* 寺 *Temple*

1	bù	不	NOT
	jř	知	KNOW
	Syāng	香	FRAGRANCE-
	Jī	積	-ACCUMU-
			LATED
	Sż	寺	TEMPLE
2	shù	數	SEVERAL
	lǐ	里	MILES
	rù	入	ENTER
	yún	雲	CLOUDY
	fēng	峯	PEAKS
3	gǔ	古	OLD
	mù	木	TREES,
	wú	無	NO
	rén	人	PEOPLE
	jìng	徑	PATH
4	shēn	深	DEEP
	shān	山	MOUNTAINS,
	hé	何	SOME
	chù	處	PLACE
	jūng	鐘	BELL
5	chywán	泉	SPRING
	shēng	聲	SOUND
	yè	咽	CHOKED BY
	wēi	危	TOWERING
	shŕ	石	ROCKS

WANG WEI (701–761 A.D.) was a member of the same generation that produced Li Bai and Du Fu. He was not only a great poet, but a great painter, a devout lay Buddhist, and a high government official as well.

"In his poems there are paintings, and in his paintings there are poems," wrote Su Shr, the Sung Dynasty poet, painter, Buddhist, and government official.

FRAGRANCE-ACCUMULATED TEMPLE 香積寺 was in the hills south of the capital. "Fragrance Accumulated" 香積 was the name of the Buddha of a mythical world where everything is made of fragrance.

This poem is about spiritual ignorance and its suppression. For Buddhists, the Enemy is not Evil, but Ignorance.

Wang Wei is ignorant of the temple, and wanders into the hills looking for it. He is lost on a deserted path when he hears the temple bell some-

6	r̀	日	SUN	where deep in the mountains.
	sè	色	COLOR	From ignorance, the poem
	lěng	冷	CHILLED BY	passes on to suppression: the
	chīng	青	GREEN	sound of a little stream is
	sūng	松	PINES	choked by the rocks. Sunlight

is screened by the pines.

7	báu	薄	THIN
	mù	暮	EVENING,
	kūng	空	EMPTY
	tán	潭	POOL
	chyū	曲	BEND

Finally, the poem's point becomes explicit: ignorant passions are subdued by meditation and the mind is made clear as a limpid pool.

8	ān	安	SETTLED
	chán	禪	MEDITATION
	jr̀	制	SUBDUES
	dú	毒	POISON
	lúng	龍	DRAGON

The Chinese believed there was a dragon in every lake and stream. The POISON DRAGON 毒龍 is a symbol of the mind's dangerous ignorance and passion.

49. Seeing Off a Monk Returning to Japan

Following cause
And effect you came
To live in the High Nation,
Your path
Like a journey in dreams.

You floated up to heaven
From afar
Across the blue sea.
Now, in the light boat
Of the Buddha's teachings
You leave the world.

Moon in the water
Learns the stillness
Of meditation.
Fishes and dragons
All listen
To your holy chants.

I just cherish
The light of your one lamp
Across ten thousand miles
Still bright to my eyes.

CHYEN CHI 錢起
Tang Dynasty
About 750 A.D.

送 *Seeing Off*　歸 *Returning to*
僧 *Monk*　　日
　　　　　　本 *Japan*

1	Shàng	上	SUPREME
	Gwó	國	NATION,
	swéi	隨	FOLLOW
	ywán	緣	CAUSES
	jù	住	DWELL IN
2	lái	來	COME
	tú	途	PATH,
	rwò	若	LIKE
	mèng	夢	DREAM
	syíng	行	TRAVEL
3	fú	浮	FLOAT
	tyēn	天	HEAVEN,
	tsāng	蒼	BLUE
	hǎi	海	SEA
	ywǎn	遠	DISTANT
4	chyù	去	GO FROM
	shř	世	WORLD,
	fǎ	法	DHARMA
	jōu	舟	BOAT
	chīng	輕	LIGHT
5	shwěi	水	WATER
	ywè	月	MOON
	tūng	通	UNDERSTANDS
	chán	禪	MEDITATION
	jì	寂	STILLNESS

The words 日本 JAPAN mean "sun origin." Japan lies off the northeastern coast of China, toward the rising sun. The Japanese claim descent from the sun-goddess.

Japan formally entered the Chinese world around 600 A.D., when the Japanese sent an envoy to the Chinese court. In the centuries that followed, many Japanese came to the SUPREME NATION to learn its arts and culture, and especially to study Buddhism.

Many things we think of as typically Japanese originated in China—Zen Buddhism, Japanese writing, styles of art and architecture. But the Japanese gave their foreign imports a distinctive Japanese flavor, just as they are doing now with imports from the West.

Buddhism teaches that things happen by CAUSE 緣 and effect, not by chance, fate, or act of God.

The word DHARMA 法 ("Buddha's teachings") refers

6	yú	魚	FISH
	lúng	龍	DRAGONS
	tìng	聽	LISTEN TO
	Fàn	梵	SANSKRIT
	shēng	聲	SOUNDS

7	wéi	惟	ONLY
	lyén	憐	CHERISH
	yī	一	ONE
	dēng	燈	LAMP
	yǐng	影	IMAGE

8	wàn	萬	TEN THOU- SAND
	lǐ	里	MILES
	yěn	眼	EYES
	jūng	中	-IN
	míng	明	BRIGHT

to the laws of existence preached by the Buddha in India around 500 B.C. The Indian word *dharma* was translated into Chinese as 法 *fa*, "law."

MEDITATION 禪 *chan* is the Chinese rendering of the Indian word *dhyana*. *Dhyana* is the state of clarity and awareness that can be reached through meditation.

SANSKRIT 梵 is the ancient Indian language in which many Buddhist scriptures are written. Chinese monks chant the original Sanskrit texts.

In one of the scriptures, it is written: "ONE LAMP 一燈 lights a hundred thousand lamps, and the darkness is made bright, and the brightness never ends."

50. *Going to Look for Master Chang of South Stream*

Everywhere along the path
In the moss,
I see the prints
Of clogs.

White cloud
Rests upon a quiet islet.
Fragrant plants
Block an idle door.

I see the color of the pines
After rain.
Following the mountain,
I reach the source of the stream.

Flowers by the water
Give Zen's meaning.
Facing them
I forget all words.

> LYOU CHANG-CHING 劉長卿
> Tang Dynasty
> About 750 A.D.

尋	*Seeking*	常 *Chang*
南	*South*	*Tao-*
溪	*Stream*	士 *-Master*

1	yī	一	WHOLE
	lù	路	PATH
	jīng	經	PASS-
	syíng	行	-WALK
	chù	處	PLACES

2	méi	莓	MOSS
	tái	苔	
	jyèn	見	SEE
	jī	屐	CLOGS'
	hén	痕	PRINTS

3	bái	白	WHITE
	yún	雲	CLOUD
	yī	依	RESTS UPON
	jìng	靜	QUIET
	jŭ	渚	ISLET

4	fāng	芳	FRAGRANT
	tsău	草	GRASSES
	bì	閉	BLOCK
	syén	閒	IDLE
	mén	門	GATE

5	gwò	過	AFTER
	yŭ	雨	RAIN,
	kān	看	SEE
	sūng	松	PINES'
	sè	色	COLOR

A TAO-MASTER 道士 is one who understands the Tao 道 (pronounced *Dau*) or "Way." In Taoism, the Tao is the basic principle of existence, the Reality that runs through all things. When Buddhism came to China, it used the same word for its own basic teachings.

CHANG 常 is the recluse's religious name. The word means "constant," "lasting," "eternal."

CLOGS 屐 are wooden clogs with two high runners, like Japanese *geta*.

The mere visual appearance of Chinese characters is not usually significant. In line 4, however, it is. The words 芳草 FRAGRANT GRASSES both contain the element ⺿ "plant," "vegetation." The words 閉閒門 BLOCK IDLE GATE all contain the element 門 "gate." One can actually see the grasses on the gate 門.

As we saw in the previous two poems, the word 禪 (here

6	swéi	隨	FOLLOW
	shān	山	MOUNTAIN,
	dàu	到	REACH
	shwěi	水	WATER'S
	ywán	源	SOURCE

7	syī	溪	STREAM
	hwā	花	FLOWERS
	yǔ	與	GIVE
	Chán	禪	ZEN
	yì	意	IDEA

8	syāng	相	TO THEM
	dwèi	對	FACING,
	yì	亦	ALSO
	wáng	忘	FORGET
	yén	言	WORDS

translated ZEN) refers to meditation, and to the state of clear awareness that meditation can bring. But it became as well the name of the "meditative" or ZEN sect of Buddhism, which arose in China during the Tang period.

This word 禪 is pronounced *chan* in modern Mandarin Chinese. During Tang, however, it was pronounced something like *zan*. The Japanese, who learned about it then, pronounce the word *zen*. Our word Zen comes from the Japanese.

Zen Buddhists believe in sudden enlightenment by direct perception of the true nature of things.

Because the true nature of things can only be seen directly, to understand it, you must FORGET WORDS 忘言 .

51. *Written after Drinking Wine*

I built my shack
Amid the haunts of men,
And yet there is no noise
Of horse or carriage.

You ask,
"How can this be?"—
Any place becomes secluded
When the mind is far away.

I pluck chrysanthemums
By the eastern fence.
In the distance
I see the mountains to the south.

The light on the mountains
Is lovely at sunset,
Flocks of birds
Fly back together for the night.

In this
There is an intimation of Truth.
I want to express it,
But have forgotten all words.

> TAU CHYEN 陶潛
> Six Dynasties Period
> About 400 A.D.

1 jyé	結	CONSTRUCT
lú	廬	SHACK
dzài	在	IN
rén	人	PEOPLE
jìng	境	REGION
2 ér	而	BUT
wú	無	THERE IS NO
chē	車	CARRIAGE
mǎ	馬	HORSE
sywān	喧	HUBBUB
3 wèn	問	ASK
jyūn	君	"SIR
hé	何	HOW
néng	能	CAN
ěr	爾	THUS"
4 syīn	心	HEART
ywǎn	遠	DISTANT,
dì	地	PLACE
dż	自	THEREFROM
pyēn	偏	OUT OF THE WAY
5 tsǎi	採	PICK
jyú	菊	CHRYSAN- THEMUMS
dūng	東	EASTERN
lí	籬	FENCE
syà	下	BELOW

Chinese poets drank quite a bit. They drank simply for pleasure and conviviality, but they also used wine as a kind of psychedelic drug—to break the veil of ordinary consciousness that conceals Reality. As Li Bai wrote:

Two cups
And I understand
   the Great Tao.
One gallon
And I am united with Nature.

TAU CHYEN (365–427 A.D.) was China's first great nature-poet. At the age of thirty-three, he gave up seeking a career in government and retired to his small estate in the country.

He is known as a "field and garden" poet, because of the pastoral scenes he described. His younger contemporary Sye Ling-yun (see poem 8) wrote about larger, wilder scenes, and is called a "mountain and water" poet.

Tau was friendly with both Buddhist and Taoist priests, but there is little overt religios-

6	yōu	悠	DISTANT-
	rán	然	-LY
	jyèn	見	SEE
	nán	南	SOUTHERN
	shān	山	MOUNTAINS

7	shān	山	MOUNTAIN
	chì	氣	AIR,
	r̀	日	SUN
	syī	夕	AT EVENING
	jyā	佳	FINE

8	fēi	飛	FLYING
	nyǎu	鳥	BIRDS
	syāng	相	EACH OTHER
	yǔ	與	WITH
	hwán	還	RETURN

9	tšz	此	THIS
	jūng	中	IN
	yǒu	有	THERE IS
	jēn	眞	TRUTH
	yì	意	IDEA

10	yù	欲	WISH TO
	byèn	辯	EXPRESS,
	yǐ	已	ALREADY
	wáng	忘	FORGET
	yén	言	WORDS

ity in his poems. He just wanted to live a peaceful, happy life. This has endeared him to generations of Chinese readers.

Two of his greatest admirers were the Sung poetess Li Ching-jau and her husband. In poem 39 she alludes to Tau when she "drinks wine by the eastern fence" and speaks of chrysanthemums, which were Tau's favorite flowers.

The word 氣 AIR ("light") basically means "breath" or "air," but can also refer to the aura or atmosphere around something, to its general "air."

EXPRESS 辯 refers to making a point in debate. Tau wants to define truth in words, but truth is beyond words.

The ancient Taoist philosopher Chuang-tzu (pronounced *Jwāng-dž*) wrote: "The purpose of a snare is to catch a rabbit. Once you have the rabbit, you forget the snare. The purpose of words lies in their meaning. Once you have the meaning, you FORGET THE WORDS 忘言 ."

52. Dwelling by a Stream

I have long been tied
By the hat-pin and seal-cord
Of an official.
Fortunate now
This banishment to the southern wilds.

At leisure
I keep to the neighborhood
Of the farmers' plots,
Looking just like
A dweller in the woods and mountains.

The morning plow
Turns the dewy grass.
At night, an oar
Scrapes the rocks of the stream.

In my comings
And goings I meet no one,
But sing long
To the blue southern sky.

LYOU DZUNG-YWAN 柳宗元
Tang Dynasty
About 805 A.D.

谿 *Stream*
居 *Dwell*

1	jyŏu	久	LONG TIME
	wéi	爲	WAS
	dzān	簪	HAT-PIN
	dzŭ	組	SEAL-CORD
	lĕi	累	TIED
2	syìng	幸	FORTUNATE
	tsž	此	THIS
	Nán	南	SOUTHERN
	Yí	夷	BARBARIAN
	jé	謫	BANISHED
3	syén	閒	AT LEISURE
	yī	依	KEEP TO
	núng	農	FARMERS'
	pŭ	圃	PLOTS
	lín	鄰	NEIGHBOR-HOOD
4	ŏu	偶	EXACTLY
	sž	似	RESEMBLE
	shān	山	MOUNTAIN
	lín	林	FOREST
	kè	客	GUEST
5	syău	曉	DAWN
	gēng	耕	PLOW
	fān	翻	TURNS
	lù	露	DEWY
	tsău	草	GRASS

Chinese gentlemen lived between two ideals: the conventional ideal of government service, and the private ideal of the cultured recluse.

LYOU DZUNG-YWAN (733–819 A.D.) was a literary prodigy whose talent helped him rise quickly in the civil service. But he was part of a reform faction that held power for a few months in 805 and then was ousted, its members exiled to the far reaches of the empire.

Lyou was exiled to the far south, a BARBARIAN region whose natives were only just learning to be Chinese.

When he says his exile is "fortunate" he is just trying to comfort himself. For us, however, it really was fortunate. During a decade of enforced idleness, he became one of Tang China's greatest prose masters. And his landscape poetry became more and more imbued with the spirit of Zen.

But Lyou once said he accepted only the part of Buddhism that was consistent with

6 yè	夜	NIGHT
bàng	榜	OAR
syǎng	響	SOUNDS
syī	谿	STREAM
shŕ	石	ROCKS
7 lái	來	COME
wǎng	往	GO,
bù	不	NOT
féng	逢	ENCOUNTER
rén	人	PERSON
8 cháng	長	LONG
gē	歌	SING
Chǔ	楚	CHU
tyēn	天	SKY
bì	碧	BLUE

the teachings of Confucius. In 815 he got the chance to turn from the reclusive ideal of the Buddhists and Taoists back to the Confucian ideal of service.

He was recalled to the capital, then sent even farther south, but this time with the rank of a local governor. He threw himself into the task of bringing Chinese culture and morality to the hill people. He repaired the local Confucian temple, fought against child-slavery, and restored Buddhist worship in a temple that had been used for human sacrifice.

He died in office in 819, having fulfilled each of the two great ideals in its time.

53. *Snowy River*

A thousand mountains
Where birds have ceased to fly.
Ten thousand pathways
Where tracks of men are gone.

A solitary boat,
An old man in reed cloak, bamboo hat—
Fishing alone
On the cold river in the snow.

LYOU DZUNG-YWAN　柳宗元
Tang Dynasty
About 810 A.D.

江 *River*
雪 *Snow*

1	chyēn	千	THOUSAND
	shān	山	MOUNTAINS,
	nyǎu	鳥	BIRDS
	fēi	飛	FLYING
	jywé	絕	ENDED
2	wàn	萬	TEN THOUSAND
	jìng	徑	PATHS,
	rén	人	PEOPLE'S
	dzūng	踪	TRACKS
	myè	滅	OBLITERATED
3	gū	孤	SOLITARY
	jōu	舟	BOAT,
	swō	簔	REED CLOAK
	lì	笠	BAMBOO HAT
	wēng	翁	OLD MAN
4	dú	獨	ALONE
	dyàu	釣	FISHES
	hán	寒	COLD
	jyāng	江	RIVER
	sywě	雪	SNOW

This is LYOU DZUNG-YWAN'S most famous poem. It is like a painting, and became the inspiration for many later poems and paintings.

The most important word in the first two lines is one that is not there: "snow." Chinese critics say this makes the snow seem even more pervasive.

The scene unrolls like a Chinese painting, revealing one layer at a time: snowy mountains—empty paths—solitary boat—old man fishing—snowy river.

"The twenty words make twenty layers, yet the poem is all of one piece," wrote a Chinese critic.

Hidden in the poem is Lyou's view of himself as a lonely outcast, frozen out in a cold world. He wrote it during his years of exile.

54. *Encountering Snow, I Spend the Night with a Host on Lotus Mountain*

Evening,
Deep in green mountains.
The weather is cold,
This thatched hut is poor.

Out at the gate
Of rough brushwood
A dog barks.
Someone comes home
On this night
Of wind and snow.

LYOU CHANG-CHING 劉長卿
Tang Dynasty
About 750 A.D.

遇	*Encounter*	芙	*Lotus*
雪	*Snow*	蓉	*Mountain*
宿	*Spend Night*	山	
		主	*Host*
		人	

1	r̀	日	DAY
	mù	暮	AT EVENING,
	tsāng	蒼	GREEN
	shān	山	MOUNTAINS
	ywǎn	遠	DISTANT
2	tyēn	天	SKY
	hán	寒	COLD,
	bái	白	THATCHED
	wū	屋	HUT
	pín	貧	POOR
3	chāi	柴	BRUSHWOOD
	mén	門	GATE,
	wén	聞	HEAR
	chuǎn	犬	DOG
	fèi	吠	DARK
4	fēng	風	WIND
	sywě	雪	SNOW,
	yè	夜	NIGHT
	gwēi	歸	RETURNS
	rén	人	PERSON

Wandering in the mountains, the gentleman LYOU CHANG-CHING (709–780 A.D.) is cut off by a snowstorm and forced to seek shelter in a poor mountain hut.

This poem is less "beautiful" than the previous one, but it has a special immediacy, a Zen-like sense of Reality directly perceived. Lodging in a strange place, insecure among rough peasants and the storm, the poet suddenly hears a dog barking in the night.

THATCHED 白 literally means "white." It refers to the white grasses traditionally used in China as thatching material.

A BRUSHWOOD GATE 柴門 is a gate woven of small branches and twigs or of strips of bamboo.

Notice the element 犬 DOG in the character 吠 BARKS. The 口 is a mouth.

55. Night Rain

An early cricket chirps
And then is silent.
The dying lamp goes out,
Then flares again.

Outside the window
I know there is rain
In the night.
From banana leaves
First comes the sound.

BAI JYU-YI 白居易
Tang Dynasty
About 800 A.D.

夜 *Night*
雨 *Rain*

1 dzău	早	EARLY
chyúng	蛩	CRICKET
tí	啼	CHIRPS
fù	復	AND AGAIN
syē	歇	PAUSES
2 tsán	殘	DYING
dēng	燈	LAMP
myè	滅	GOES OUT
yòu	又	AND AGAIN
míng	明	IS BRIGHT
3 gé	隔	ON THE OTHER SIDE OF
chwāng	窗	WINDOW,
jī	知	KNOW
yè	夜	NIGHT
yŭ	雨	RAINING
4 bā	芭	BANANA
jyāu	蕉	PLANT,
syēn	先	FIRST
yŏu	有	HAS
shēng	聲	SOUND

As a Chinese poem, this is nothing special. In fact, its formal parallelism obscures what it really has to say.

The poem brings us face to face with Reality: the Reality of a cricket chirping and the sound of rain on a late summer night twelve hundred years ago. These are somehow the same Reality you or I are living at this instant.

The haiku anthologist and Zen eccentric R. H. Blyth called this poem "pure haiku" and "pure poetry."

Here poetry becomes a means of liberation. The Nature that is what it is, nothing more and nothing less, reveals itself in all its common glory.

56. Deer Fence

In the empty mountains
I see no one,
But hear the sound
Of someone's voice.

Slanting sunlight
Enters deep forest,
And shines again
On green moss.

WANG WEI 王維
Tang Dynasty
About 700 A.D.

鹿 *Deer*
柴 *Fence*

1 kūng	空	EMPTY
shān	山	MOUNTAIN
bù	不	NOT
jyèn	見	SEE
rén	人	PERSON
2 dàn	但	ONLY
wén	聞	HEAR
rén	人	PERSON
yǔ	語	SPEAKING
syǎng	響	SOUND
3 fǎn	返	RETURNING
jǐng	景	SUNLIGHT
rù	入	ENTERS
shēn	深	DEEP
lín	林	FOREST
4 fù	復	AGAIN
jàu	照	SHINES
chīng	青	GREEN
tái	苔	MOSS
shǎng	上	UPON

DEER FENCE 鹿柴 was a fence of woven brushwood where deer congregated on Wang Wei's estate.

This is a poem of jewels: simple, gem-like characters and solid objects on the one hand, murmuring voices and reflected light on the other.

"Form is emptiness, emptiness is form." The physical world and the void of enlightenment are one and the same.

SOUND 響 can also mean "echo."

RETURNING SUNLIGHT 返景 is the light of the afternoon sun, which has fallen low enough that its slanting rays again penetrate the forest.

Chinese poems seldom use personal pronouns such as "I," "you," or "he." Their absence helps give this poem its air of mysterious impersonality.

57. *Seeking the Recluse*

Beneath the pines
I inquired of his servant,
Who said, "My master has gone
Picking herbs.

"He is in these mountains
Somewhere,
But the clouds are deep,
And I do not know where."

JYA DAU 賈島
Tang Dynasty
About 800 A.D.

尋 *Seek*　　　　　不 *Not*
隱 *Hidden-Away*　遇 *Come Upon*
者 *Person*

1	sūng	松 PINES
	syà	下 BENEATH,
	wèn	問 ASKED
	túng	童 SERVANT
	dž	子 BOY
2	yén	言 SAID:
	shr̄	師 "MASTER
	tsǎi	採 PICKING
	yàu	藥 MEDICINAL
		HERBS
	chyù	去 GONE
3	jr̆	祇 ONLY
	dzài	在 IS LOCATED
	tsž	此 THESE
	shān	山 MOUNTAINS
	jūng	中 AMID
4	yún	雲 CLOUDS
	shēn	深 DEEP,
	bù	不 NOT
	jr̄	知 KNOW
	chù	處 PLACE"

JYA DAU (779–849 A.D.) was a wandering monk who gave up the religious life for a life among worldly poets. But he still understood the mystery and joy of living hidden away in the mountains.

Many Chinese MEDICINAL HERBS 藥 grow high in the mountains.

Like Li Bai's "Question and Answer in the Mountains" (poem 1), this is a simple, flowing poem that uses the language of everyday speech.

The poem's beauty is hard to explain. Somehow, in its simplicity and pointlessness, it is like Nature.

There is a Chinese saying that the best lines of poetry are made by Heaven, but it takes a great poet to discover them.

Chinese Pronunciation

The Chinese language developed independently of any Western language. That being so, it is surprising how few of its sounds are strange to us.

One thing that does seem strange is the fact that each word must be pronounced with a specific tone of voice. The syllable *ma* can have four meanings, depending on what tone is used in pronouncing it—*mā* means "mother," *má* means "hemp," *mǎ* means "horse," *mà* means "to curse":

> The first tone, *mā*, is high and level   ≣
> The second tone, *má*, is high and rising   ≣
> The third tone, *mǎ*, dips low and then rises   ⩎
> The fourth tone, *mà*, starts high and falls   ⩏

These are the tones of modern Mandarin Chinese. Other dialects and previous ages had somewhat different sets of tones. Tang Chinese had one level tone, one rising tone, one falling tone, and a short, sharp tone.

Most of the transliterated Chinese words in this book are written according to the Yale romanization system. A few words I have left in their more common spellings—for example, Peking, Szechwan.

You can achieve a reasonable approximation of Chinese pronunciation by following these rules:

a as in c*a*rt
  ai as in *ai*sle
  au between *au*thor and *ou*t.
e as in al*e*rt
  ei as in w*ei*gh
  ye as in *ye*t
  ywe as in "Are *y'we*t?"
  wen as in *won*.

i as in rav*i*ne.

o as in c*o*rd

   ou as in s*ou*l.

u as in t*oo* (e.g., *tu*)

   or in t*oo*k (when followed by a consonant, e.g., *tung*).

yu as in *you* (more precisely, like the German *ü*—round your lips
to say *oo*, but say *ee* instead).

the *r* in *chr, jr,* and *shr* and the

   z in *sz* and *dz* are buzzing sounds.

ts at the beginning of a word is hard for many people to pronounce:
tsai is like c*at's eye*.

The next step in improving your pronunciation is to get a
language tape from a library or bookstore.

Selected Bibliography

1. A Basic Library

Liu, James J. Y. *The Art of Chinese Poetry.** University of Chicago Press, 1962. An introduction to Chinese poetics.
Liu, Wu-chi, and Irving Yucheng Lo. *Sunflower Splendor.** Garden City, N.Y.: Doubleday Anchor, 1975. An enormous collection of dependable translations of poems from all periods.
Watson, Burton. *Chinese Lyricism: Shih Poetry from the Second to the Twelfth Century.** New York: Columbia University Press, 1971. An excellent short history of the most common form of Chinese verse.

2. General Works

Owen, Stephen. *Traditional Chinese Poetry and Poetics: Omens of the World.* Madison: University of Wisconsin Press, 1985. Interesting ways of thinking about Chinese poetry.
Payne, Robert, ed. *The White Pony: An Anthology of Chinese Poetry from the Earliest Times to the Present Day.* New York: John Day, 1947; Mentor, 1960. Loose and inaccurate translations, many of which are vivid and moving.
Rexroth, Kenneth. *One Hundred Poems from the Chinese.** New York: New Directions, 1959. Poems by Du Fu, Su Dung-pwo, Li Ching-jau, Lu You, and others, translated in his own easy manner by a major American poet.
——— and Ling Chung. *The Orchid Boat: Women Poets of China.** New York: McGraw-Hill, 1973.
Waley, Arthur. *Chinese Poems.** London: Allen & Unwin, 1946/1961/1982. One of the masterworks of the man some think the greatest translator of all.
Watson, Burton, tr. and ed. *The Columbia Book of Chinese Poetry, From Early Times to the Thirteenth Century.* New York: Columbia University Press, 1984. An intelligent selection of uniformly good translations.

* Available in paperback

3. Ancient Times

Hawkes, David. *Ch'u Tz'u; The Songs of the South.* Oxford: Clarendon Press, 1959. Shamanistic and other poetry of southern China.

Karlgren, Bernhard. *The Book of Odes.* Stockholm: Museum of Far Eastern Antiquities, 1950. Chinese text and dependable translation of the Book of Songs.

Pound, Ezra. *The Classic Anthology as Defined by Confucius.* Cambridge: Harvard University Press, 1954. Peculiar and inaccurate, but fascinating version of the Book of Songs.

Waley, Arthur. *The Book of Songs.** London: Allen & Unwin, 1937; New York: Grove Press, 1960; Merritt Linn, 1982. Still the standard translation.

4. Six Dynasties

Birrell, Anne. *New Songs from a Jade Terrace: An Anthology of Early Chinese Love Poetry.* London: Allen & Unwin, 1982.

Davis, A. R. *T'ao Yüan-ming (A.D. 365–427): His Works and Their Meaning.* Cambridge University Press, 1976.

Frodsham, J. D. *The Murmuring Stream: The Life and Works of Hsieh Ling-yün.* Kuala Lumpur: University of Malaya Press, 1967, 2 vols. Sye Ling-yun. The first volume is biography and translations, the second is notes.

―――― and Hsi Ch'eng. *An Anthology of Chinese Verse: Han Wei Chin and the Northern and Southern Dynasties.* Oxford: Clarendon Press, 1967.

Holzman, Donald. *Poetry and Politics: The Life and Work of Juan Chi (A.D. 210–263).* Cambridge University Press, 1976. Rwan Ji.

5. Tang

Bynner, Witter, and Kang-hu Kiang. *The Jade Mountain: A Chinese Anthology.* New York: Knopf, 1929; Doubleday Anchor, 1964; Vintage, 1972. This is a translation of the "Three Hundred Tang Poems," an eighteenth-century collection that is the most popular book of poetry in China.

Frodsham, J. D. *The Poems of Li Ho.* Oxford: Clarendon Press, 1970. Also published as *Goddesses, Ghosts and Demons: The Collected Poems of Li He (790–816).* Berkeley, Calif.: North Point Press, 1983.

Fusek, Lois. *Among the Flowers: The Hua-chien Chi.** New York: Columbia University Press, 1982. Beautifully direct translations of pre-Sung song-lyrics.

Graham, A. C. *Poems of the Late T'ang.** Baltimore: Penguin, 1965. Vivid translations of Du Fu, Du Mu, Li He, and others, by the greatest British translator since Waley.

176

Hawkes, David. *A Little Primer of Tu Fu*. Oxford: Clarendon Press, 1967. Du Fu's poems in the original Chinese, with word-by-word translations and commentary.

Hung, William. *Tu Fu: China's Greatest Poet*. Cambridge: Harvard University Press, 1952; New York: Russell and Russell, 1969. Critical biography with translations.

Kroll, Paul. *Meng Hao-jan*. Boston: G. K. Hall, 1981. Critical biography of Meng Hau-ran, with translations.

Nienhauser, William H., et al. *Liu Tsung-yüan*. New York: Twayne, 1973. Critical biography of Lyou Dzung-ywan, with translations.

Owen, Stephen. *The Great Age of Chinese Poetry: The High Tang*. New Haven: Yale University Press, 1981. Biographies, history, criticism, and translations.

———. *The Poetry of the Early Tang*. New Haven: Yale University Press, 1977. Tang poetry before the golden age.

Robinson, G. W. *Poems of Wang Wei*.* Baltimore: Penguin, 1974.

Stimson, Hugh M. *Fifty-five Tang Poems: A Text in the Reading and Understanding of Tang Poetry*. New Haven: Far East Publications, Yale University, 1976. Language textbook. Includes original pronunciations.

Wagner, Marsha L. *Wang Wei*. Boston: Twayne, 1981. Critical biography with translations.

Waley, Arthur. *The Life and Times of Po Chü-i*. London: Allen & Unwin, 1949. Reprinted 1970. Critical biography of Bai Jyu-yi, with translations.

———. *The Poetry and Career of Li Po*. London: Allen & Unwin, 1950. Critical biography of Li Bai, with translations.

6. SUNG

Hu, P'in-ch'ing. *Li Ch'ing-chao*. New York: Twayne, 1966. Critical biography of Li Ching-jau, with translations.

Lin, Yutang. *The Gay Genius: The Life and Times of Su Tungpo*. New York: John Day, 1947; Westport, Ct.: Greenwood Press, n.d. Imaginative biography of Su Shr by the inimitable Lin Yutang.

Liu, James J. Y. *Major Lyricists of the Northern Sung*. Princeton University Press, 1974. Song-lyrics with Chinese text, modern pronunciation, word-by-word translation, and commentary.

Rexroth, Kenneth, and Ling Chung. *Li Ch'ing-chao: Complete Poems*.* New York: New Directions, 1979.

Watson, Burton. *The Old Man Who Does as He Pleases: Poems and Prose by Lu Yu*. New York: Columbia University Press, 1973. Works by Lu You.

———. *Su Tung-p'o: Selections from a Sung Dynasty Poet*.* New York: Columbia University Press, 1965. Poems by Su Shr.

Yoshikawa, Kojiro. *An Introduction to Sung Poetry*. Translated by Burton

Watson from the Japanese. Cambridge: Harvard University Press, 1967. Penetrating history of Sung poetry, with translations.

7. OTHER WORKS

Birch, Cyril, ed. *Anthology of Chinese Literature.* New York: Grove Press, 1965, 2 vols. The best general anthology of Chinese poems, essays, stories, plays, historical writing, etc.

Blyth, R. H. *Haiku: Vol. I, Eastern Culture.** Tokyo: Hokuseido, 1949. Paperback edition South San Francisco: Heian International, 1981. Blyth's entertaining but profound four-volume *Haiku* is one of the great books of the twentieth century. This first volume includes a section on Chinese poetry as a formative influence on Japanese haiku.

Hightower, James Robert. *Topics in Chinese Literature: Outlines and Bibliographies.* Cambridge: Harvard University Press, 1953. Revised 1966. Excellent outline history of Chinese literature, though the bibliographies are not up-to-date.

Liu, Wu-chi. *An Introduction to Chinese Literature.* Bloomington: Indiana University Press, 1966. The standard university text.

Newnham, R., and Lin Tung. *About Chinese.** Baltimore: Penguin, 1980. Introduction to the Chinese language.

Schirokauer, Conrad. *A Brief History of Chinese and Japanese Civilizations.* New York: Harcourt, Brace, Jovanovich, 1978. A good short history.